1880 CENSUS:

BLEDSOE COUNTY, TENNESSEE

Transcribed by:

Byron Sistler and Barbara Sistler

JANAWAY PUBLISHING, INC.
Santa Maria, California

1880 Census: Bledsoe County, Tennessee

Originally printed, Evanston, Illinois
1980

Reprinted by

Janaway Publishing, Inc.
732 Kelsey Ct.
Santa Maria, California 93454
(805) 925-1038
www.JanawayGenealogy.com

2007, 2013

ISBN: 978-1-59641-165-4

Made in the United States of America

IMPORTANT INFORMATION

<u>You cannot utilize the material in this booklet at all effectively unless you read the</u>
<u>following.</u>

This booklet is an exact transcription of the county schedule, household by household. A
transcription in sequence from the schedules is very useful in placing the relationships
of neighboring families. When the county by county transcription is completed, a state-
wide index of heads of household and of individuals whose surnames differed from that of
the household head will be prepared to be used either with the printed transcriptions or
the microfilm.

Surnames appear in capitals. Where a surname does not appear before the person's given
name in a family listing he has the same surname as the entry immediately preceding him.
Given names were copied as read with the exception of Francis--Frances to indicate sex of
person. Where there is a doubt about gender of a name we have followed it with (m) or (f).

Age of each person is listed after his name. Unless indicated by (B) (Black) or (Mu)
(Mulatto), the person is Caucasian (W). In a household, unless a symbol for race appears
after a name, person is of same race as the preceding household member(s).

Occupations were shown on the schedules for all persons but young children. These are
listed in our transcription with the following exceptions--farmer or farm labor for men and
housekeeping for females. Thus, if no occupation is given, farmer or housekeeeper can be
assumed.

Illnesses and infirmities at time of the census enumeration are shown as indicated on the
schedules.

The place of birth of each individual was to be included on the schedules along with place
of birth of each of his parents. We have used standard Post Office abbreviations for the
states, except where Tennessee is indicated we simply use a T. If the individual and both
parents were born in Tennessee this item is omitted. Also in households where the parents
were born in other states but the children were born in Tennessee the birthplaces of the
father and mother are not repeated unless there is a discrepancy.

Relationship of all persons in the household to the head of household was to be indicated.
We have omitted this where it was obvious that the second person was the wife and succeed-
ing individuals were the offspring of the father. Where identification in this fashion
seemed unclear we entered what we thought were appropriate notations.

An example from the transcription (fictitious entry) should be informative:

> SHELTON, George 47 (T AL GA), Susan 37, Bettie 20, Narcissa 18, Mary 15
> (KY), Ada 13 (blind); WALKER, Caroline 40 (sister) (widow) (T AL GA),
> George 21 (nephew); MAXWELL, Eli (B) 35 (farmhand), Louisa 28
> (servant); SCRUGGS, Henry 28 (W) (boarder) (schoolteacher), Josie
> 24 (Henry's wife), Mamie 3 (Henry's dau)

This translates into George Shelton age 47, a white man born in Tennessee whose father was
born in Alabama and mother in Georgia; his wife Susan age 37, born in Tennessee and
parents also born in Tennessee; George's children Bettie, Narcissa, Mary and Ada. The
first two were born in Tennessee, Mary in Kentucky and Ada in Tennessee. Ada is blind.
George's sister Caroline Walker lives with the family with her son George (though con-
ceivably George Walker is not Caroline's child). A black man, Eli Maxwell, lives here and
works as a farmhand for George Shelton. Louisa Maxwell, listed as servant, is probably
Eli's wife, but she could be a sister. The Henry Scruggs family is made rather clear in
the schedules, as noted above; they were Caucasian.

Keep in mind that this is a copy from handwritten schedules. Although the condition of
the schedules and the handwriting is much improved in 1880 over earler censuses, it is
still quite possible to misinterpret individual names (or letters).

Byron & Barbara Sistler

Hh#	Page 1, Dist. 1

1. McREYNOLDS, Henry (B) 52 (NC SC __), Mariah 42 (T NC __)
2. LEDBETTER, John (B) 50 (GA NC GA), Polly Ann 27 (wife) (T __ T), Wade 8, Sarah 5, Flora 3, Eliza 1
3. McREYNOLDS, Benj. 62 (B) (T __ __), Annie 55? (VA __ __), Margaret 16
4. PONSON?, Jack (Mu) 26 (VA __ __), Mariah (B) 20
5. DUKE, Benjamin A. 54 (cooper) (T __ __), Elizabeth 43
6. HASKEW, Adam V. B. 44 (T __ __), Nancy F. 41, William J. 18, Talitha A. J. 14, Sarinda E. 12, Joseph A. V. B. 7
7. PUTNAM, George V. 35 (AL T __)
8. PUTNAM, Mary 33 (AL T __), Franklin V. P. 13 (T __ __)
9. PEMBERTON, Constant (m) 58 (VA VA __), Lucinda 56 (T NC __); VARNS, Arvanzina 13 (g dau) (FL FL __), William M. 12 (g son) (T FL __), James 9 (g son) (T FL __)
10. JONES, Azleteen 27 (f), Cora E. 2 (dau)
11. WHITTENBURG, Joseph T. 30 (T __ __), Mary 25 (T NC __), Florence 9, James 26 (bro) (T __ __), John 17 (nephew) (T __ T); LAWSON, James 3 (nephew) (T __ T)
12. FERGUSON, Elisha 33 (T __ __), Mary 30 (prolapsus utori) (T __ __), Alice J. 9, James McT. 7, Minnie N. 5, William R. 3, David E. 4/12 (b. Jan)
13. PUTNAM, James M. 38 (AL T __), Sarah E. 28 (T T __), John H. 10, Mary H. 8 (AR), James H. 3 (T), Gertie R. 8/12 (b. Sep)

	Page 2, Dist. 1

14. FERGUSON, Charles 39 (T KY NC), Margaret J. 38, Julia Ella 16, Walter 6, Mary Ann 4, Hallie 1
15. CREECH, Richard 79 (NC NC NC), Delila C. 47 (wife) (NC NC NC)
16. BLEVINS, Squire 65 (NC __ NC), Mary 56 (VA VA VA), John 22, William 18, Squire 17, Franklin 11; CLARK, Susanne 34 (dau) (tayloress), Mary 15 (g dau) (T __ T), McDONALD, James 26 (servant) (T __ __)
17. JOHNSON, Warren 63 (CT CT CT), Martha Jane 25 (wife) (T NC VA), Elizabeth 11 (dau), William F. 4, Minnie 2
18. CREECH, Benedict 25 (VA NC NC), Martha J. 22, James A. T. 2/12 (b. Mar); SIMPSON, Charles R. 6 (stepson) (T __ T)
19. ANDERSON, Louiza 35 (widow) (tayloress) (VA NC NC), John B. 10 (T T VA)
20. HALE, John 50 (T __ T), Susan J. 33 (wife), Amande J. 15, Sarah E. 13, John 6, Ira 3, Lucius 1
21. HALE, Burrell 35 (T __ T), Sarah J. 36, Nancy A. 16, Martha N. 14, James A. 10, Eliza Jane 7, Lily Ann 3; SKILLEM, Nancy M. E. 27 (boarder); DUKE, Matilda 7 (boarder) (T __ T)
22. WHITE, Clarisa 66 (widow) (NC NC NC), WHALEY?, William L. L. 19 (g son)
23. _____, Lewis 25, Mary 22 (T __ __), Franklin? 1, _____, _____ (detail obliterated)

	Page 3, Dist. 1

24. CAGLE, Littleton 27 (T NC T), Sarah E. 22, Frances A. 4, Ida E. 2, Emmett 6/12 (b. Nov); TETERS, William 16 (servant)
25. DOUGLAS, Missouri 45 (T __ NC), Elizabeth 34 (T __ T), John 9, Clarisa E. 5, Thomas 3, William M. 7/12 (b. Oct)
26. DOUGLAS, John 50 (NC __ NC), Amanda 48 (T __ __), Thomas 9, Alexander 1, James 5 (g son) (T __ T); BLAYLOCK, Isaac 2 (g son) (TX __ T)
27. GOINS, Rebecca (Indian) 36 (T T __), Reilly 15, Elvira 13, Clavin 9, Mahala 5, Hattie 2, Orpha 63 (mother in law) (W) (T __ __)
28. GOINS, Matilda (Indian) 25 (T __ __), John 6 (son), Hester A. 2 (dau); KING, Jane 14 (niece) (T __ T), Thomas 18 (nephew) (T __ T)

Hh#	Page 3 (cont'd)

29. GOINS, Isabella (Indian) 26 (T T __), James 8 (son), Angeline 6 (dau), Emiline 6 (dau), Mary 4 (dau), Henry 2 (son), Matilda 10/12 (b. Jul) (dau)
30. DUKE, Melinda 50 (divorced) (T __ __)
31. LAWSON, David 48 (T __ __)
32. BROCK, Jesse 58 (torpid liver), Nancy E. 36 (wife), Samantha E. 14, Amanda E. 13, Jesse W. 11; WHALEY, Sarah 18 (servant) (cook)
33. JOHNSON, Thomas 45 (T T AL), Martha 25 (wife) (KY KY KY), Robt. W. 1 (KY T AL)
34. TURNER, Thos. 37 (T NC VA), Mary 32 (T __ T), Sarah J. 10, Martha M. 9, Eli 7, Mary E. 6, Ida E. 2

	Page 4, Dist. 1

35. COX, John W. 31 (T NC T), Amanda 23 (T __ T), Celia E. 5, William 4, Minnie 1
36. HICKEMBOTTOM, Celia 55 (T NC NC)
37. TURNER, John 39 (T NC GA), Nancy 28 (T __ T), Henry 12, Thomas 8, William 5, Eliza 1
38. SUTHERLAND, John 56 (T NC T), Elizabeth 48 (T SC SC), Nancy J. 14, John T. 11, Eliza A. 10
39. SONGER, David 60 (stone mason) (VA VA VA), Anna 46 (torpid liver) (T __ T), William F. 25 (scrofula), Rachel C. 21, John L. 19, Mary E. 9 (g dau)
40. JOHNSON, James 35, Mary 25 (T __ __), Lucinda 8, Annie 4, Victor 2
41. HOLLAND, David 25, Margaret 26 (debility)
42. HOLLAND, Robert 57 (T __ VA), Susan 56 (SC __ __), James M. 23, John S. 22, Sarah A. F. 20; DILL, Joseph 12 (servant) (T __ __)
43. JOHNSON, William J. 37, Rhoda S. 29 (T __ T), William E. 11, James A. 9, Annie 6, Charles W. 1
44. HITCHCOCK, Wilburn 23, Dianna 24, John M. 3, Franklin L. 1

	Page 5, Dist. 1

45. JOHNSON, William 60, Martha 39 (wife), Nancy 24 (dau), Samuel 21, Thomas 16, Wyley 13, Caleb 10, Joshua 7, Dolly 3
46. RUSSELL, John J. 59 (T NC NC), Omy J. 50 (wife) (T NC NC), John N. 19, James B. 16, William E. 13 (diarhea), Henry L. 10 (scrofula)
47. OWINGS, Edward S. 65 (T NC NC), Lydia E. 57 (NC NC NC), Morgan W. 17
48. HITCHCOCK, James 70 (T NC MD), Charlotte 60 (T KY T), Alfred 23, Jabes 20
49. HITCHCOCK, James D. 25, Susan E. 24 (T __ __), Florence W. 2/12 (b. Mar)
50. HALE, William 26, Nancy A. 39, Charles 8 (chorea sineti viti), America 7, Vesta C. 4, Frances E. 3, Alice 2, Buck 4/12 (b. Jan)
51. HOLLAND, David 55 (T T __), Elizabeth J. 34 (wife) (sick headache), William R. 21 (son) (T T __), John E. 9 (T T T), James 6, Aaron A. 4, Julia A. 1; HICKENBOTTOM, William B. 18 (g son) (rheumatism) (T VA T)
52. RICHARDSON, Leroy 31 (T __ __), Nelly 25 (T T __), Nancy E. 7, Sarah F. 2; HOLLAND, Kitty 23 (sis in law) (T T __)
53. JOHNSON, John 23, Mary A. 25, Eliza E. 1

	Page 6, Dist. 1

54. RAINEY, Annie C. 50 (widow), William J. 24, Eliza J. 18, Clora E. 14, John S. 13, Marilda C. 10
55. HOLLAND, Joseph 24 (married within yr), Sarah A. 20
56. HOLLAND, William 43 (T T __), Nancy E. 40 (T __ __), Sarah Jane 21, James A. 17, William L. 14, Zachary 18 (cousin)

Hh#	Page 6 (cont'd)

57. RUSSELL, John (Indian) 40 (NC NC NC), Sarah (W) 39 (wife) (T SC T), John 19, William 12, Dura P. 12, Bersheba E. 9, James 7, Juda 5, Emma 3, Babe 3/12 (b. May) (m) (these children all listed as Indian)
58. KEENER, William 27, Eliza 26; SONGER, Frances 7 (step dau); KEENER, John 2 (son), Wayman T. 2/12 (b. Mar)
59. SNIDER, James D. 33, Elizabeth 33 (GA __ __), Sarah J. 5, Henry J. 3, Ninney M. 2
60. WHITE, William S. 45 (T __ T), Melinda J. 38, Berry L. 12, Anderson C. 10, Fanny M. B. 5, Alida E. 1, Benjamin D. 18 (son), Laura Lee 16 (dau); FLYNN, Mary E. 21 (step dau), Rebecca A. 18 (step dau)
61. FORD, Ira 52 (Canada VT NY), Elizabeth 41 (PA PA PA), Walter 14 (MI), Charles 10 (MI)
62. KEENER, Jackson 55 (T NC T), Rachel 54 (T __ T), Terry 19 (son), Mary 17, Fanny 15, Alaxander 12, Harvey 9, Elizabeth 7 (g dau), Sarah 4 (g dau)

Page 7, Dist. 1

63. COLVARD, Sarah 45 (widow), William A. 15 (son) (T NC T), H. Posey 11, Thad 8, Florence 6, Delila 3
64. CHILDRESS, Joseph M. 26, Martha 25, John T. 10, Mary M. 8, William E. 6, Annie 3, James H. 1
65. GRIFFETH, Thomas J. 48, Spicy 61 (wife), Nora 12 (niece)
66. HARVEY, James C. 52 (T SC VA), Elizabeth 55 (T SC SC)
67. BAGGETT, Drura B. 50 (AL __ __), Matilda A. 30 (T VA VA), Louiza T. 11, James M. 8 (KY), Cordelia E. 6 (KY), David L. 4 (KY), Martha A. 4 (KY), Iula C. 1 (T)
68. SMITH, Isaac N. 37 (T SC SC), Martha 40 (T T __), John 13, Louis B. 11, Aaron T. 8, Joseph E. 6, James J. 3, Charles 4/12 (b. Feb)
69. SMITH, James M. 54 (T SC T), Catherine 48, Andrew J. 19, James T. 16, Sarah A. 14, Minnie A. 5
70. SMITH, George W. 24, Margaret P. 19 (T NC T), Arthur 3, James P. 1

Page 8, Dist. 1

71. SMITH, Noah 27, Martha 25, Lawrence 5, Luther 3, James F. 1/12 (b. May)
72. CHILDERS, John A. 21 (T NC T), Minny J. 18 (T NC T), Martha E. 1
73. DeBORD, John W. 50 (VA VA VA), Joanna 48 (VA VA VA), John W. 15, Thomas M. 10, Norman S. 2
74. PENNINGTON, Francis 22, Martha E. 20 (T VA VA), Thadeus W. 3, Joanna A. 8/12 (b. Sep)
75. CHILDERS, Adaline 56 (widow) (T __ __), James 17 (T NC T), Leander P. 15, Ada V. 11
76. HUMBLE, Andrew J. 24, Clara M. 22 (T NC T), Clarles (sic) A. 5, James S. 3, Ulysses G. 11/12 (b. Jun)
77. COLVARD, Wiley M. 45 (NC NC NC), Virginia 34 (T AL VA), Mary 9, Gordon 6, James 3, William 8/12 (b. Nov)
78. BRIDGMAN, Samuel (Mu) 36 (T __ NC), Sally 26 (T __ GA), Delphia 8, Charles F. 5, William A. 3, Ersa 5/12 (b. Dec)

Page 9, Dist. 2

79. TURNER, Solomon 55 (T SC VA), Eveline 39, Kansas 24 (dau), John 17, George 15, Thomas 12, Samuel 4, Robert 2, Pocahontas 9, Calhoun 1/12 (b. Apr)
80. SMITH, John G. 52 (T SC T), Melissa 40 (T VA NC), George 17, Catharine 7, Thomas 5, Joseph A. 4, Isaac N. 2, Andrew J. 1; BEDWELL, Martha 78 (mother in law) (NC NC NC)
81. DeBORD, Mary 62 (widow) (VA __ VA), Andrew 34 (VA VA VA)
82. DeBORD, Abijah 24 (T VA VA), America 20, Samuel F. 6/12 (b. Nov)

Hh#	Page 9 (cont'd)

83. DeBORD, Martin 23 (T VA VA), Mary A. 21 (T NC T), Charles F. 1
84. SMITH, John 24, Nancy M. 18 (GA __ __), Ada V. 1
85. FRASIER, Saml. P. 39, Nancy E. 35 (T NC NC)
86. WARD, John W. 32 (T NC NC), Mary I. 29 (T __ __), Matilda J. 10 (phthysic), James E. 7, Clarence E. 5, Dorene M. 3, Albert E. 1
87. WHITTENBURG, Peter 28, Laura 21, Ada 5 (dau), Ota 1 (dau)
88. ACUFF, Jonathan 71 (widower) (T __ __), Ornetta A. 19 (dau) (T T NC), Emily M. 21, Jonathan 17
89. ACUFF, James 33 (carpenter) (T T NC), Margaret A. 28, Emmett E. 13, James W. 10, Charles R. 8, Sarah E. 6, Laura L. 4, Thomas D. 3, Robert B. 1

Page 10, Dist. 2

90. WARD, Jonathan S. 40 (OH CT NY), Nancy E. 27 (wife) (OH PA NY), Francis H. 3
91. KNIGHT, Andrew C. 28 (T NC T), Mary 27, Minny V. 7, Ulysses 6, Laura L. 5, Ada E. 3, John 1
92. HEMPHILL, Samuel C. 57 (merchant) (OH KY VA) Mary C. 44 (NY NY NY), Maud 7 (MI), Paul 5 (T), Frank 4, Ida 3, Elizabeth 1; ALDRICH, Ellen C. 15 (step dau) (MI Can NY), Emma 14 (MI Can NY)
93. MARTIN, Absalom 60 (T VA VA), Elizabeth 55 (T VA VA)
94. BLANKINSHIP, Gilford G. 40 (VA VA VA), Nancy M. 33, James D. 12, Elizabeth C. 9, Absalom B. 7, Mary F. 5, William H. 2
95. MEDLEY, James 52 (NC __ NC), Jane E. 36 (wife) (T NC NC), Sarah 15 (dau) (T NC NC), James H. 11 (T NC T), Harriet M. A. C. 9 (T NC T), Isaac C. 7 (T NC T), Charles E. 6 (T NC T), Joseph A. 4 (T NC T), Minny Belle 2 (T NC T)
96. MORSE, Charles H. 45 (ME MA MA), Lizzie M. 42 (ME ME ME), Emma M. 19 (DC), Hartwell M. 16 (CT), Lizzie B. 14 (MA), Helen L. 12 (MA)
97. FRADY, Baxter W. 24 (NC NC NC), Martha V. 20, Polly 40 (mother) (NC __ NC), Elizabeth A. 18 (sis) (GA NC NC)

Page 11, Dist. 2

98. MILUM, John A. 52 (T VA VA), Martelia M. 39 (wife), William P. 17, Mary A. 16, Lilly May 7, Charles H. 4, Alice Lee 2
99. MERRIMAN, Lowry M. 35 (T NC NC), Martha A. 28, John F. 13, Josephine 11, Annette 9, Ida 7, Luther 5, Lilly 3
100. BEACH, Sampson L. 28 (T NC NC), Mandeville M. 21 (wife) (T __ __), Ida E. 1
101. WALLING, Noah 24, Sally 19, Harvey 1
102. HOPKINS, Isaac 64 (NC __ __), Mary 54 (T __ __), Eliza J. 32, Fanny 26, Isaac C. 2 (g son) (T __ T); McJUNKIN, Thadeus T. 46 (relationship omitted) (T __ __), Martha A. 51 (NC __ VA), Margaret L. 16, William S. 13, Sherman C. 10
103. FRASIER, William G. 21 (T __ __), Elizabeth P. A. 25 (T T NC)
104. TURNER, William 25, Palistine 21 (wife) (GA SC SC), Charles 5 (son), Jesse 2, Martha 9/30 (b. May)
105. HALE, John I. 22 (T T __), Sally 21, Martha J. 2, Samuel P. 10/12 (b. Jul)
106. ROLLINS, Daniel 52 (T SC SC), Louiza J. 53 (NC __ __), JoLany? 21, Martha A. 18, Margaret J. 16, George W. 11, George W. 72 (bro) (SC SC SC)

Page 12, Dist. 2

107. BEACH, Oliver C. 67 (NC NC NC), Selah 76 (wife) (NC NC T), Rula M. 43, Robert L. 9 (g son)

Hh#	Page 12 (cont'd)

108. BEDWELL, Andrew J. 50 (T T NC), Louiza J. 37 (wife) (T NC NC), Catherine E. 18, Mary 17 (KY), James F. 14 (KY), John O. 11 (T), Charles S. 9, Andrew J. 6, Sarah A. 3

109. WHITE, Isaac E. 47 (T VA T), Ruth L. 41 (VA VA VA), George T. 15, Emma J. 14, Daily E. 12, John L. 8, Giles A. 7, Ruth L. 4, Ally W. 1 (dau)

110. WHITE, John P. 49 (T VA T), Caroline 45 (VA VA VA), Minnie E. 20, Isaac L. 19, John L. 18, Conelia A. 16, Horace M. 14, Jeremiah D. 12

111. WHITE, Daniel 78 (VA ___), Elizabeth M. 38 (wife) (VA NC NC), Caroline M. 2

112. MARTIN, James H. 26, Tabitha I. 30 (tayloress) (T NC NC), Willie S. 2, Babe 3/12 (b. Mar) (dau)

113. MOORE, James M. 21, Lucinda A. 21, Mary E. 5/12 (b. Jan)

114. FRADY, George McD. 20 (married within yr) (NC NC NC), Nancy J. 18; KNIGHT, Elizabeth 75 (g mother) (T Holland T)

115. WILLIAMSON, Vavassor A. G. 24 (NC NC NC), Sarah C. S. J. 18 (T __ T)

116. WILLIAMSON, William M. 53 (NC NC NC), Emma 54 (NC NC NC), Mary A. V. 21 (NC), James B. J. 19 (T), William B. 17, John L. M. 14

Page 13, Dist. 2

117. FRASIER, John 67 (widower) (T NC NC), Amy E. 34 (dau) (T NC T), Sarah F. 17 (dau) (T NC T); WARD, Nancy M. 15 (g dau) (T __ T)

118. SIMMONS, Thomas 25 (T NC NC), Fanny C. 25 (T ___); MASON, Elizabeth 37 (sis in law) (T __ __), John A. 2 (nephew) (T T)

119. HOPKINS, Jesse M. 53 (T __ __), Nancy 45 (T VA VA), Beersheba E. 10, Eliza C. 7, Isaac C. 4

120. MOONEYHAM, Owen B. 38 (widower) (T NC SC); PANEY, Amelia C. 26 (servant) (T __ __)

121. ANGEL, Jackson 52 (NC T T), Martha L. 47 (T NC NC), Laura J. 24 (T __ __), Mary A. 20 (T T T), John 17, Josephine 15, Angeline 13, Eliza Ann 11

122. RIDLEY, Alaxander 56 (GA __ __), Elizabeth D. 42 (GA __ __), Fanny V. 10, Nancy A. 7; MOORE, Rachel V. 52 (servant) (T VA)

123. TURNER, Joseph 21 (T __ __), Mary M. 19 (T T)

124. ANGEL, William 48, Rachel 40 (T __ __), James 20, Nancy A. 16, Armina 13, Peter 11, Lucresa 8, Charles 7 (dau?), Ferrell 4, Bird 3/12 (b. Feb) (son), Wiley 14

125. MARSH, Terrell 30 (T __ NC), Sarah J. 40 (wife) (T T VA), Elizabeth 66 (mother) (NC NC NC)

126. CREASON, Jasper 35 (T NC KY), Sarah 23 (wife), Nancy J. 13, Martha A. 10 (T T), Lucinda 5 (T __ T), James A. 7 (T __ T), Lucius J. 8/12 (b. Sep) (T __ T)

Page 14, Dist. 2

127. SMITH, James M. (Mu) 48 (T __ __), Sarah J. 48 (W) (T T SC), Monroe 4 (stepson)

128. WARD, John L. H. 72 (NC NC NC), Matilda 71 (NC VA NC), Albert N. 24 (son); HILL, John W. 12 (bounden) (T __ __)

129. PANTER, Alexander 47 (T T VA), Susan 37, Lilly A. 13, Mary V. 12, John 9, Samuel 7, Sarah 4, Theola 1

130. KNIGHT, Franklin M. 36 (T NC T), Mary 34 (T GA MS), Nancy J. 12, James N. 10, Harmon T. 8, Adelia A. 5, Lilly May 3, Andrew T. 4/12; BEACH, John 6 (nephew)

131. MOONEYHAM, Lucinda 56 (widow) (T __ __), James W. 24, Sarah P. 19

Hh#	Page 14 (cont'd)

132. SEALS, James 74 (rheumatism) (NC VA VA), Elizabeth 64 (T VA T), Solomon 25

133. BLAYLOCK, William A. 28 (T NC T), Elva Jane 23 (T NC T), Nathaniel 3, James T. 11/12 (b. Jun)

134. LAWSON, Wesley 56 (T T __), Sarah 49 (T NC SC), Joseph A. 27, Mary A. 21, William R. 21 (nephew) (T T __)

135. LAWSON, Jesse 50 (T __ __), Clementine 43 (T T __), George F. 12, Sarah E. 4, Florence May 2/12 (b. Mar); SIMMONS, Thomas 19 (stepson), Belle S. 16 (step dau)

Page 15, Dist. 2

136. SIMMONS, William T. 40 (T NC NC), Elizabeth 27 (wife) (T VA VA), Sampson 17 (son), Mary 13, James 11, Joseph 9, Rebecca 6, Edith 4, Bertha 17/30 (b. May) (T T __)

137. TERRY, Mary Jane (B) 57 (T __ Africa)

138. SIMMONS, Andrew 38, Julia E. 30, Sarah E. 5, Mary L. 3, James T. 1; COLLINS, William J. 7 (nephew) (T KY T)

139. SIMMONS, James 41, Hetty 40; COLLINS, Zachary T. 10 (nephew) (T KY T)

140. SEALS, James Jn. 30 (T VA T), Martha 36 (wife), Bellzora 11, Seburn 9, Coda 7 (son), Franklin 5, Howard 4, Nancy Ann 3/12 (b. Feb)

141. SEALS, Zela 38 (T VA T), Rebecca 26 (wife), Joseph L. 5, Lucinda E. 2, Daniel F. H. 4/12 (b. Jan)

142. SEALS, James 53 (T VA T), Nancy Ann 45 (T NC T), Jane 24, William 6, Nancy E. 4, John 7/12 (b. Oct); SIMMONS, James R. 18 (stepson), Martha A. A. 11 (step dau); ERVIN, N. P. 9 (stepson); BARBER, Sarah B. 27 (dau), James E. 1 (g son) (T IL T), SEALS, Mary E. B. 1 (g dau) (T __ T)

143. FARMER, Alexander F. 31, Loiza C. 30, Samuel K. 9, Clarence E. 8, Nicrotia V. 5, Amy Rosetta 2

Page 16, Dist. 2

144. PEARSON, Thomas D. 59 (NY Eng NY), Lavinia 46 (NY NY NY); PRATER, Darcus J. 9 (servt dom) (MO T T)

145. KNIGHT, Jane 69 (widow) (T VA VA); SEALS, Sarah J. 48 (dau) (T NC NC), James T. 7 (g son)

146. CHILDERS, Mary 34, Eliza Jane 6/12 (b. Nov) (dau)

147. MOORE, John 36 (NC NC NC), Melinda 35 (NC NC NC), Nancy C. 14 (NC NC NC), Jesse 12 (NC), Amanda 10 (KY), John 8 (T), Laura 5, Orissa 1/12 (b. Apr)

148. HOPKINS, Margaret 53 (T NC NC)

149. FERGUSON, William H. 36 (T __ T), Mary M. 32 (T NC T), John Hen. 12, James H. 10, William R. 8, Sidney A. 3/12 (b. Feb)

150. MOORE, Nancy A. S. 24 (T NC __), Alaxander H. 9/12 (b. Aug) (son) (T __ T)

151. POE, William 67 (GA GA GA), Fanny M. 40 (wife) (GA GA GA), Sarah C. 21 (GA), Lewis McM. 19 (GA), Josephine 17 (GA), Magdaline M. 3 (g dau) (T T GA), William T. 2 (g son) (T __ GA)

152. FREEMAN, Bird 50 (T T NY), Sarah 52 (T NY T), JAMES, Willis (Indian) 78 (dependent) (paralysis) (SC VA SC)

153. FREEMAN, James M. 38 (T T NC), Armina 30 (NC NC NC), Robert A. 11, James G. 9, Rachel E. 7

154. SIMMONS, John 50 (T NC SC), Drucilla 42 (T T VA), Adaline 22, Abraham 18, Mary 16 (KY), Margaret 13 (KY), James M. 10 (IL), Eurassus 7 (T), Elmos E. 4, Reuben M. 2, Clarisa 70 (mother) (SC NC NC)

3

Hh#　　　　Page 17, Dist. 2

155. BLACKBURN, Robert G. 47 (T NC T), Melissa C. 45 (T T NC), Robert C. 23, Elbert S. 21, Francis A. 18, Jesse E. 17, Marquis G. 13, Lula May 10, Margaret A. 39 (sis) (tayloress) (T NC T)
156. CREASON, William 64 (NC __ VA), Lucinda 72 (wife) (KY VA VA)
157. HALE, Thomas S. 31 (T __ __), Patience K. 35 (T __ T), Mary Ann 12, Isaac W. 7, John T. H. 3, Sarah S. E. 1
158. WALKER, Isophine (f) 50 (T __ __), Samuel 10 (son) (T __ T); SINGLETON, Fanny 45 (sis) (T __ __), Thomas 8 (nephew) (T T)
159. PRATER, Elizabeth 37 (widow) (T __ __), George W. 19 (son) (MO __ T), John 17 (MO __ T), Nancy E. 11 (MO __ T), Willie 6 (MO __ T), James T. 2/12 (b. Mar) (T __ T)
160. GRAHAM, William R. 32, Margaret E. 23 (MI NY NY), Albert S. 1, David C. 25 (bro)
161. CRAWFORD, Jonathan H. 42, Fanny J. 43, Elizabeth 13, John F. 11, Thomas E. 9, James R. 19 (bro)
162. CRAWFORD, Mary 45, Wyatt E. 11 (son) (T __ T), Nancy J. 9, Melissa E. 7, Benjamin C. 3/12 (b. Feb)
163. FOSTER, Julia Ann 65 (T __ __)
164. BLAYLOCK, Richard 63 (NC __ __), Jane 46 (wife) (T __ __), Allie C. 23 (dau), James J. 21, John M. 15, Fanny J. 13, Mary A. 11, Levina M. 4, Austin R. 2, Nancy Jane 5 (g dau), Sarah E. 3/12 (b. Feb) (g dau)

Page 18, Dist. 2

165. SULLIVAN, Isaac 32, Margaret 23, Elizabeth 7, Samantha 4, Angeline 1; SMITH, Elizabeth 45 (mother in law), Arminta 13 (sis in law), Etheldridge 69 (wife's g father) (T NC NC)
166. BLAYLOCK, Thomas F. 37 (T NC NC), Nancy 27, John F. 7, Jesse B. 5, Lucretia E. 3, James M. 1
167. JONES, Franklin 25 (T NC T), Sarah E. 22, Albert Lee 5/12 (b. Dec), William 71 (father) (cooper) (gravel) (NC NC NC)
168. SMITH, William B. 45 (T NC T), Nancy J. 40 (T __ NC), Joanna 15 (dau), Rebecca A. 12, Mary E. 6, Harmon R. 1
169. SMITH, John P. 36 (T NC T), Nancy 18 (wife), James W. F. 2
170. BLAYLOCK, Frances J. 57 (widow) (NC NC NC), John 36 (T VA NC), Emiline 22, Angeline 20, Elijah 18
171. BLAYLOCK, Jesse 30 (T VA NC), Tennessee 25 (T __ __), Samuel 1
172. BOYNTON, Lewis 43 (ME ME ME), Orissa M. 34 (ME ME ME), Alonzo B. 13 (ME), Martie M. (f) 10 (ME), Frank A. 7 (ME), Susie B. 1 (ME)
173. McDONALD, William 49 (widower) (NY NY NY), William K. 21 (MN NY OH)
174. HOUSTON, William 38 (T GA NC), Martha A. 31, Burvada 9 (dau), James H. 8, Olly J. 6 (dau), Lucy Ann 5, George W. 3, Lizzie 1

Page 19, Dist. 2

175. HOUSTON, Delilah 77 (NC __ __)
176. WARNER, Alfred 47 (T __ KY), Caroline 44 (T __ __), Martha E. 17, Terrena 15 (dau), George H. 13, George W. 13, John R. 10, Andrew 8, Amelia 6, Viola 2
177. CLARK, Francis M. 52 (T __ __), Mary C. 41, Euphemie 12
178. LOYD, Benjamin F. 43, Caroline J. 35, Mary E. 13, Delilah J. 11, John H. 8, William F. 6, Martha J. 4, Sarah S. 2, Benjamin R. E. 3/12 (b. Feb)
179. GREER, David 44 (OH PA PA), Harriet E. 40 (NY NY __), Frank A. 19 (MI), Fred J. 16 (MI), Bertha May 10 (MI); FULLER, Dientha 87 (mother in law) (NY __ __)

Hh#　　　　Page 19 (cont'd)

180. WALKER, David H. 64 (VA VA VA), Rhoda 60, Jane 22; HALE, Sarah 19 (dau) (married within yr)
181. WALKER, Mathew 24 (T VA T), Nancy 28, Melinda J. 5, Selah Ann 3, William D. 1
182. MOYERS, Albert H. 35 (widower), Matilda C. 14, Brent 13, Parilee 10, Biron 8, Minnie 5, Cansada 4

Page 20, Dist. 2

183. MOYERS, George A. 75 (T VA T), Martha 72 (T NC PA)
184. MOYERS, George L. 29 (T __ __), Harriet H. 30, Larriet A. C. 11 (dau), Aaron 8, Levina J. 6, Orissa E. 3, Olla V. 8/12 (b. Sep) (dau)
185. WYATT, John 52 (NC NC __), Martha 43, Sabrina J. 19, Jacob D. 16, Joseph R. 13, John L. 11, Rosie A. 8, William J. 5, Herschel R. 2; MOYERS, Daisy I. 1 (niece)
186. BREWER, Elizabeth 59 (widow) (VA NC VA), Nancy 26 (T T VA), George W. R. 17
187. BREWER, Pleasant A. 21 (T T VA), Nancy E. 19, Henry E. 2, Mary A. 2/12 (b. Mar)
188. PERRY, Oliver H. 29 (widower) (NY VT NY), BLODGETT, Louisa M. 48 (mother) (divorced) (NY MA NY)
189. AIKIN, Posey 35 (GA SC NC), Sarah 28 (MO T T), Nancy A. 11, Martha L. 7, Mary J. 5, Manerva E. 3, William M. 9/12 (b. Aug)
190. BREWER, Pleasant B. 30 (T NC NC), Manerva C. 27 (T SC NC), James M. G. 11, William L. 8, Pleasant M. 6, Ephraim P. 3, John B. 1
191. MAYNARD, Fanny 45, Missouri E. J. 14, John D. 8, Charles T. 5; BREWER, Elizabeth 77 (mother) (NC NC NC)
192. STEPHENS, Andrew (Mu) 54 (T VA VA), Millie Ann 47 (KY KY KY), Mary E. 10, William H. 8, Martha A. 5; SWAFFORD, Rachel (B) 76 (mother) (VA VA VA)

Page 21, Dist. 2

193. EDMONDS, John R. 26, Mary 16 (wife), Ellison 1
194. WALKER, Stephen 45 (carpenter) (T VA T), Mary Ann 49 (KY __ KY), James H. 24, Alexander M. 21, William S. 14; MORRIS, Drucilla C. 27 (cousin) (tayloress) (T VA VA)
195. WORTHINGTON, Reuben 45, Angeline 30 (wife), Fanny J. 11, Elizabeth 9, Mary 7, James 4, Reuben 1
196. EDMONDS, Jordan 54 (widower), William B. 22, Pleasant A. 19
197. STONE, Patrick L. 32, Mary 24, Caldonia 4, Monrovia D. 3, Babe 2/12 (b. Mar) (son)
198. MOYERS, George A. 25 (carpenter & stone mason), Susan A. 30, Florence 8, Martha 6, James 4, Reuben 4, Babe 2 (dau)

Page 22, Dist. 3

199. SMITH, James H. 53 (KY KY KY), Martha A. 52 (T T NC), Nancy 19 (T), William G. 16 (KY), Lavina 13 (KY), Martha A. 10 (T); CARTRIGHT, William 71 (father in law) (T __ __)
200. HARDIN, Nancy 36 (widow) (T T NC), William R. 13 (KY __ T), Lemon N. 6 (T), Lafayette 2 (T)
201. SWAFFORD, Henry (B) 30 (T __ GA), Sally (Mu) 27 (T NC T), Margaret 15 (step dau) (T __ T), Lizzie 12 (step dau) (T __ T), John 9, Charlotte 6, Jennie 4, Ada 1; COOK, Chany C. 75 (mother in law) (T __ __); SWAFFORD, Alexander 7 (son)
202. AGEE, Thomas 36 (MO T T), Sarah 32, Florence 12, Jennie 10, Elizabeth 8, Samuel 6, Ada 4, Thomas 1
203. SWAFFORD, Peter J. 69 (SC SC SC), Tennessee 28 (wife) (tayloress) (T VA T), Mary Jane 6, Charles R. 5, James B. 3

Hh#   Page 22 (cont'd)

204. VICKREY, Peter J. 22, Lucy A. 24, Lilly C.
     2, Robin 7/12 (b. Oct) (son)
205. SWAFFORD, Alaxander (B) 55 (NC __ __), Mary
     A. (Mu) 22 (wife) (T __ __), Asbury 17,
     George M. 16, Matilda 14, Charles 11,
     Willie 6/12 (b. Nov)
206. SWAFFORD, Mary E. 45 (widow) (KY KY KY),
     Lucretia 20 (T T KY), Isaac E. 18,
     John P. 15, Virginia E. 13, Charles 9,
     Minerva A. 7

Page 23, Dist. 3

207. RANKIN, Henry 30 (Mu), Adaline E. 23 (T __
     VA), Sylva I. 5, Eliza E. 3, Bula V.
     4/12 (b. Jan)
208. BROWN, Reuben H. 46 (T __ T), Joanna E. 23
     (wife) (T T KY), James 8, Milo 2
209. BALLARD, Joseph G. 33 (GA __ __), Elizabeth
     32 (T VA T), Nancy C. 12, Flora J. 9,
     James M. 6, Samuel D. 4, Pearly E. 1;
     RECTOR, Jesse 22 (servant)
210. SWAFFORD, David (B) 27 (T SC __), Sarah A.
     28 (T VA VA), Mary E. 5, George A. 2,
     William 2/12 (b. Mar)
211. SWAFFORD, Eliza 60 (widow) (T NC T), William
     B. 40, Christiana 36, Thomas A. 34;
212. THURMAN, Richard (Mu) 53, Rebeca (B) 35 (T
     VA VA), Ellen (Mu) 15, Sylva 14,
     Gather (m) 11, Ross 6, Martha 4, George
     3, Babe 3/30 (b. May) (son)
213. PULLEN, Agga (f) 35 (T VA NC), Mary 15 (dau)
     (T __ T), Rebecca 10, Florence G. 7,
     Lenora 4, Hester 2 (flux), Rebecca 42
     (sis) (T VA NC)
214. WALKER, Elizabeth 45 (widow) (T T VA),
     James 20, Sally 17, Luverna 14, Mossy
     9 (g dau) (T __ T)

Page 24, Dist. 3

215. BOSTON, William C. 39 (cooper) (KY NC T),
     Manerva C. 39, William H. H. 19 (T KY
     __), Wyley 14 (T KY T), Mary J. 13,
     Martha E. 11, Isaac 6, Violet J. 4,
     Zo. Caroline 2, Harriet 6/12 (b. Nov)
216. SWEAT, George M. 37, Susan 39 (T VA VA),
     Lucy E. 15 (KY), George W. 13 (T),
     Martha E. 10, John P. 5
217. HYDER, Alfred 58 (carries the mail) (T __
     __), Sally 61 (T __ T), John 21,
     Elijah 17, Andrew 13; HICKMAN, Nancy
     J. 17 (step dau), Mary L. 16 (step
     dau); JONES, Sassafine 7 (step g dau)
218. FOSTER, Joshua 26 (AL __ T), Rachel 24,
     Jonah 6 (IN), Sarah B. 3 (T), John E.
     1
219. FOSTER, Ephraim H. 33 (T __ __), Melinda
     C. 27 (T KY T), Nancy A. 9, Thomas M.
     7, Amanda E. 5, James R. 6/12 (b. Nov)
220. HOUSTON, James 30 (carpenter), Kizzare 30,
     Daniel 15, Mary E. 11, John 8, Cath-
     erine 6, Manerva M. 5, James C. 3,
     Nancy J. 1
221. STEPHENS, Roll (B) 50 (VA VA VA), Catharine
     46 (T VA VA), Samuel 16, William 14,
     Clay 12 (rheumatism), Lawrence 6,
     Gather 3 (m)

Page 25, Dist. 3

111. STEPHENS, Mark 71 (T VA NY), Charlotte E.
     56 (wife) (VA VA Ire), James A. 25
223. PATTON, Elijah 42 (T __ T), Martha 34, Owen
     15, Mary Jane 13, Candace A. 11, Nancy
     A. 9, Sarah M. 7, Fielding E. 1
224. MORGAN, George W. 27, Samantha A. E. 23,
     Martha E. 5, James C. 3, Carroll V. 2,
     John E. 1/12 (b. Apr)
225. WEBB, George W. 29 (T VA T), Nancy J. 25,
     John L. 7, Mary A. 5, Martha E. 1

Hh#   Page 25 (cont'd)

226. HINCH, John C. 46 (T AL GA), Martha C. 35,
     John H. 17, Emily B. 15, Anna J. 13,
     Isaac C. 11, Gather E. (m) 9, Elizabeth
     6, Virgil 2, Ada 11/12 (b. Jun), Andrew
     J. 48; BOSTON, George W. 23 (servant)
     (T NC T); RODDY, Newton T. (B) 19
     (servant) (teacher) (T VA T)
227. TOLLETT, William (B) 60 (T GA GA), Matilda
     (Mu) 56 (T __ __), Arena A. 8;
     STEPHENS, Mary 26 (widow) (dau), Sally
     6 (g dau), Albert 4 (g son)
228. HALEY, Peter (Mu) 28 (widower)
229. BURNETT, William 55, Rebecca Ann 40 (wife),
     William T. 20, Nancy Ann 17, James F.
     16, Martha 13, Mary 10, Vincent 8, John
     C. 5, Elizzie 3, Sarah J. 4/12 (b. Jan)

Page 26, Dist. 3

230. STEPHENS, John (Mu) 23 (T VA T), Lucinda
     18, William 3, Henry 9/12 (b. Aug)
231. STEPHENS, Isaac (B) 31 (T KY VA), Carolina
     25, James W. 7, Ulysses L. 2
232. FREILEY, Mary W. 48 (widow) (teacher) (T SC
     VA), Larken E. 14 (T KY T), Nancy L. 7
233. GUESS, Richard (Mu) 40 (T __ VA), Harriet M.
     35, Mary E. 11, William H. 10, Martha
     A. 9, Annie J. 6, Samuel R. 5, George W.
     4, John L. 5/12 (b. Dec)
234. SWAFFORD, Aaron 43 (T SC T), Louiza J. 40
     (T KY KY), George W. 22, James N. 20,
     Thomas 18 (infantile paraylsis), Aaron
     16, James A. 17, Amanda E. 12, Martha 9,
     John 6, William 3; HAYES, Aaron 16
     (newphew), Henry 10 (nephew); YOUNG,
     Jesse 11 (orphan), Florinda 9 (orphan)
235. TOLLETT, Elijah G. 52 (farmer & merchant)
     (T VA VA), Nancy 50 (T NC NC), John A.
     30, Wesley 25, Craven 19, Syrene 17,
     Elijah G. 15, William 13, Mark 10,
     Moses 8; YOUNG, Melinda 16 (servant);
     ORMES, Charles (Mu) 18 (servant)

Page 27, Dist. 3

236. PATTON, Thomas 32 (T KY T), Nancy E. 32,
     William 10, Martha B. 8, Syrene 6,
     Elijah 5, Samuel W. 3, Nancy M. 1
237. AULT, George W. 31 (merchant), Vesta A. 31,
     Gertrude 2; BLUFF, Dolly (B) 11 (ser-
     vant) (T __ __)
238. HALEY, John B. 36, Martha J. 27, Rhoda L.
     9, Elijah G. 7, Mary C. 4, Harriet A. 2,
     John B. 8/12 (b. Sep); ROSE, Louiza 21
     (servant)
239. TILLEY, Edward F. 61 (NC NC NC), Eliza 55
     (T VA T), Martha J. 21, Luhany 18
240. TILLEY, John 22 (T NC T), Mary J. 21,
     Mary E. 22/30 (b. May)
241. TILLEY, Robert N. 24 (T NC T), Carrie L. 25
     (T T __), Edward L. 3, Eliza I. 1,
     Elijah 1/12 (b. Apr)
242. LITTLE, Francis M. 60 (GA __ __), Jemima 55
     (GA __ __), Polly Ann 35 (AL), Jemima
     C. 33 (AL), Martha A. 33 (AL), Cynthia
     J. 22 (AL), Rosena M. 20 (AL), Amanda C.
     18 (AL), George R. L. 16 (AL), Nancy L.
     12 (T)
243. CARTRIGHT, Semon 35 (T __ __), Martha J. 25,
     Mary 7, Eliza J. 5, Rhoda 4, Mily 1
     (dau); YOUNG, Park 26 (bro in law)

Page 28, Dist. 3

244. GOTT, Lafayette 31 (T T NC), Eliza R. 32
     (T SC SC), Charles K. 7, Arminta 5,
     Thomas R. 3, Alfred H. 1; SLOAN, John
     H. 23 (servant)
245. GOTT, Russell 68 (widower) (T MD SC), Sarah
     50 (T MD SC)
246. DAY, Jesse F. 33 (T NC T), Dicy A. 32
     (tayloress), Eliza E. 6, Catharine J. 4,
     Elizabeth 65 (mother) (T T NC)

5

Hh#	Page 28 (cont'd)

247. WORTHINGTON, Howard (Mu) 45 (VA VA VA), Jane 35 (VA __ __), Elizabeth 18, Eliza 15, Lydia A. 13, Cyndia 12, Fanny 12, John 7, William 3/12 (b. Feb), Albert 16
248. DAY, William 27, Amanda (T KY KY), Charles 5, Samuel 2, William 1/30 (b. May)
249. BRUCE, Joseph E. 21 (married within yr) (T T NC), Martha 19; GREEN, Sarah 41 (mother) (divorced) (weaver) (NC NC NC)
250. SWAFFORD, James B. 34 (married within yr) (T SC T), Mahulda A. 18 (wife), Polly Ann 68 (mother) (T GA T), Burrell R. 29 (bro) (T SC T) (epilepsy), Nancy A. 28 (sis) (T SC T), James A. 13 (nephew), Goldsboro 9 (nephew)
251. TAYLOR, Charles P. 35 (T KY KY), Emma 25, Eliza Jane 4/12 (b. Jan)
252. TAYLOR, Isaac N. 68 (miller) (KY VA NC), Elizabeth 67 (KY T VA), William G. 23, Elizabeth A. 14 (g dau), Samuel P. 16 (g son)
253. SWAFFORD, Isaac E. 25, Martha Ann 23, Salina A. 3, Sally R. 1

Page 29, Dist. 3

254. PATTON, Josiah 67 (farmer & blacksmith) (KY T T), Mahulda 50 (wife) (T NC VA), Anna J. 42 (dau) (tayloress), Jesse 21, Samuel 17, Josephine 15 (asthma), Sarah A. 12, Robert 8; TUDOR, Landon 21 (servant)
255. PATTON, Martin 28 (married within yr) (T KY T), Jennie 23
256. HOLLOWAY, William C. 52 (stone mason), Mary A. 42 (T NC VA), John 21, Joseph 16, Jesse 12, Annie 10, Belle 6, William 4
257. WATKINS, Benjamin M. 30 (makes furniture) (IN NC NC), Isabel 27 (IN IN VA), Elizabeth A. 7 (IN), Francis M. 6 (dau) (IN), Annie M. 5 (IN), Minnie L. 2 (IN), James E. 8/12 (b. Sep) (T), Hicks K. 19 !bro) (makes furniture) (IN NC NC), Melinda 55 (mother) (NC NC NC)
258. HALE, Jesse H. 22 (married within yr) (T T NC), Margaret 20 (T T __)
259. HALE, William 67 (T NC NC), Susan P. 65 (NC NC NC)
260. HALE, Alfred 26 (T T NC), Elizabeth 29 (GA GA GA), Marion T. 1 (son), Jemima B. A. 2/12 (b. Mar)
261. HALE, John R. 32 (T T NC), Martha J. 26 (tayloress), William O. 8, Alfred W. 5, Samuel J. 2, Franklin W. W. 9/12 (b. Aug)
262. LEE, Harriet (Mu) 40 (widow) (T __ T), George 17 (T __ T), Elizabeth 15 (cook), Andy 13, Mary 9
263. LEE, William 45 (T VA NC), Elizabeth 45 (T NC), Rachel E. 21, James R. 19, William B. 17, Nancy E. 15, Sarah L. 12, John 10, Israel 6, Darius 4; NAIL, Elvira 65 (cousin) (T GA T)

Page 30, Dist. 3

264. HAMILTON, John 60, Margaret 48 (wife), Elizabeth 19, Eliza J. 17, John 15, Sarah 12
265. GREER, Moses (Mu) 20
266. WADE, James M. 48 (AL VA GA), Rachel 42, Martha J. 12, Mary E. 12, James W. 10, Virginia 9, William G. 6
267. TOLLETT, Franklin 24, Sarah L. 22
268. BRIDGMAN, Oliver (B) 22 (T __ __), Sarah (Mu) 24 (T __ __), Rhoda E. 2, Fanny B. 1

Hh#	Page 30 (cont'd)

269. THURMAN, Isaac N. 42 (merchant), Sarah J. 38, William R. 17, John C. 15, Hester Ann 13, Annie J. 11, Lonidas M. 6, Landon 4, Isaac E. 9/12 (b. Aug), John (B) 20 (servant) (T T GA), Angeline 32 (servant) (T T GA)
270. HAMILTON, Isaac (Jesse?) E. 26, Martha A. 24, Sarah L. 4, Barbara E. 3; NAIL, Margaret 51 (aunt) (tayloress) (T GA T), Franklin 14 (cousin)
271. AGEE, William 39 (makes furniture) (IN T T), Ruth 33, Josie 17 (tayloress), Mary 16 (teacher), Samuel 14, Emma 10, Thomas 4, Luther 2

Page 31, Dist. 3

272. TULLUS, James E. (Mu) 40 (T VA VA), Sally 31 (tayloress) (T KY VA), Sofrona A. 15, Sarah J. 12, Mary T. 9, Flora A. 1; STEPHENS, Sally 65 (mother in law) (VA VA VA), William H. 18 (uncle), Sarah L. 16 (aunt?)
273. AULT, William H. 23 (physician)
274. BURNETT, Daniel 27 (blacksmith), Mary 24 (NC NC T), Sarah E. 6, Eliza J. 4, Mary L. 2, Andrew J. 1/12 (b. Apr); CAPPS, Margaret S. 12 (servant) (T __ __)
275. LEE, Benjamin F. 41 (T VA __), Mary E. 36 (T __ T), Hester A. 12 (T T __), James B. 10, Luhany 7, Ida B. 4, Robert O. 1
276. IVANS, Joseph A. 29, Susan 24, Arthur 3, Thomas H. 1
277. LEE, Thomas B. 23, Flora C. 20, James B. 1
278. ROBERTS, Hugh L. 50 (T NC T), Jane 46 (T SC NC, John F. 10, George E. 8, Eliza E. 2
279. BROCK, William A. 24 (T __ KY), Arminda E. 22 (Indian) (T __), Joseph 3, Caldonia 3/12 (b. Feb); LANE, Maggie J. 5 (step dau)
280. SWAFFORD, Alfred 78 (SC SC SC), Martha J. 39 (wife) (T T VA), Mary T. 7
281. CLOSE, Nancy 50 (widow) (T SC NC), Caldonia 22 (T T NC), Sally 15, Kate 15

Page 32, Dist. 3

282. SWAFFORD, Alfred K. 39 (T SC NC), Terasda 34, Hasting M. 10, Listing P. (m) 7, Walter W. 9/12 (b. Aug)
283. SWAFFORD, John 34 (T SC NC), Eva 27 (T __ NC), Lester 4, Victor H. 2, Beulah 5/12 (b. Dec) (son?)
284. MOORE, Polly A. 49 (widow) (T NC NC), John M. 17, William L. 14
285. SWAFFORD, Samuel Sn. 56 (T SC SC), Eliza E. 43 (wife) (T __ VA), Thomas J. R. 27 (son), Mary R. 21, Martha J. 18, Louis C. 17, Jesse B. 13, Hester A. 11, Robert E. A. 8, Eliza F. 5, Walter N. 3
286. KNIGHT, William 42 (NC T T), Elvira 42 (NC NC NC), Thomas L. 16 (GA), George W. 13 (GA), Lucius H. 11 (GA), Henry B. 7, William McR. 6 (T), John W. 3 (T)
287. LEE, Anderson 43 (T VA SC), Louisa J. 36 (KY T KY), Enoch G. 14 (T), Luhany E. 13 (KY), Edward A. 11 (KY), Mary Belle 9 (KY), Robert J. 8 (KY), Sherrord B. 6 (KY), Samuel W. 4 (T), Maggie A. 2 (T), Jennie O. 2/12 (b. Mar) (T)
288. SWAFFORD, Samuel Jn. 37 (T SC __), Carrie E. 31, Alice 11, Nancy E. 10, Martha J. 6, Pernada 3, Thomas Y. 2

Page 33, Dist. 3

289. SWAFFORD, Thomas Y. 74 (SC SC SC), Hannah 68 (T NC NC); WILSON, William G. 15 (g son)
290. SWAFFORD, Lucy (B) 70 (crippled) (VA __ __), George 16 (g son) (T VA T)
291. SWAFFORD, Nason 39 (T SC T), Narcissus 37 (wife), Samuel 16, China E. 14 (dau), Robert 12, James 11, Darius 9, Thomas D. 7, Joseph 4, William 2/12 (b. Mar)

Hh#   Page 33 (cont'd)

292. SWAFFORD, Alfred H. 26 (T SC T), Martha 17;
     CLARK, Thomas 17 (servant) (T __ T)
293. McMILLON, Joseph 51 (T NC T), Bethenia 50
     (T NC NC), Alice E. 18, Martha E. 15,
     Florence 13, Texana 6, Mariah 2
294. HALE, Aquilla 46 (widower) (T NC NC),
     Josephine 21, Samuel 18 (crippled),
     Martha J. 17, Thomas 15, Mary E. 14
295. WORTHINGTON, Henry (Mu) 21 (T VA VA),
     Amanda (B) 22 (T GA VA), Annie J. 1
     (Mu)
296. SWAFFORD, Clay (B) 21 (T GA __), Sarah 22
     (T VA VA), Zarina 6, Evaline 5, China
     E. 3, Emma 2, Callonda 7/12 (b. Oct)
     (dau)
297. McMILLON, Asbury 21, Edith 17, Joseph E.
     7/12 (b. Oct)
298. ROBERTS, William W. 33, Tennessee 25 (tay-
     loress) (T NC T), Flora E. 4, Florence
     A. 1

     Page 34, Dist. 3

299. BROWN, John T. 38, Mary A. 18 (wife) (NC NC
     NC), William J. 4, Elizabeth E. 2;
     ROSE, Nancy 18 (servant)

     Page 1, Dist. 4

1. SWAFFORD, Isaac E. 53 (T SC NC), Manerva R.
   54 (T NC T), Isaac E. jr. 11, Ursaline
   (B) 14 (servant), James 10 (servant);
   WORTHINGTON, Eli 24 (servant)
2. BROWN, Emiline 35 (divorced), James R. 13,
   Sarah A. 9, William (Mu) 4 (son)
3. McDOWELL, J. C. 24 (T T NC), Elizabeth 24
   (wife), Thomas W. 3, Nancy L. 1 (b.
   Feb)
4. SWAFFORD, A. E. 26, Nettie 26 (wife),
   Martha J. 6, Luther E. 4, Thomas 3,
   Aaron E. 1
5. ROGERS, Isaac 30, Manda 25, William 10
6. DYRE, J. C. 23, Nancy A. 20, James O. 10/12
   (b. Aug)
7. DYRE, Samuel 21, Joseph 16 (bro)
8. McCLELLEN, Mavia (widow), Nason 22, Lewis
   16, William 15
9. CLARK, Gilbert (B) 50 (VA VA VA), Sarah 45,
   Arminty 15
10. BRIDGMAN, Oliver (B) 24, Sarah 26, Josie 8,
    Rhoda 3, Rosa 1-6/12

    Page 2, Dist. 4

11. McGEE, Thomas 21 (T T KY), Sarah 26, Martha
    E. 2, Betsie 61 (mother) (lame?) (KY
    KY KY)
12. WORTHINGTON, C. C. 32 (T T AL), Nannie 28,
    Sallie 7, Kittie 6, Tennessee 5, S.
    Robert 2
13. MILLARD, W. D. 21, Martha E. 22 (hip out of
    place), C. Weslie 9/12 (b. Sep)
14. WORTHINGTON, S. P. 42 (T T AL), Luranie 45,
    Albert (B) 18 (servant)
15. SMITH, Luther (B) 35 (VA VA VA), Nancy 37
    (T NC T) (toothache), John 14, James S.
    (Mu) 12, Martha J. 11 (B), George H.
    10, Florence 8, Robert (Mu) 7, Luther
    J. 5, H. Adaline 1-8/12
16. McDOWELL, Luteshy? 53 (NC NC NC) (widow),
    William R. 22 (T T NC), James M. 20, M.
    Anna 18
17. SAMPSON, John (Mu) 55, Martha (W) 45,
    Mattie (Mu) 15, James 12, Samuel 10
18. WORTHINGTON, J. F. (m) 42 (T T AL)
19. ROSE, Lucindie 43 (KY KY KY)
20. THURMAN, J. C. 22, Martha 20, James 4,
    Luizy E. 10/12 (b. Jul)

    Page 3, Dist. 4

21. WORTHINGTON, M. J. 44 (occ. nothing) (T T
    AL)

Hh#   Page 3 (cont'd)

22. CLARK, Jacob 51 (blacksmith), Mary 50,
    Nettie 22, Sufronia 18, Ada 15, Jonie
    14 (son), Alice 11, Hettie 8, Crutch-
    field 23 (son), Isaac 22 (nephew) (T
    __)
23. HOGE, Preston 44, Jansoka? 47 (liver com-
    plaint), Mary 10, Martha 8, Roena 5,
    Isaac E. 3, Samuel 13 (nephew);
    SWAFFORD, R. E. 22 (stepson) (rose
    canser?), Sarah 16 (step dau)
24. CROCKET, William (B) 25 (cooks on farm) (VA
    VA VA), Martha 30, Anna Jane 8 (VA),
    Hester 5 (VA); SWAFFORD, Lidie 70 (dis-
    abled)
25. LITTLE, F. M. 32 (AL __ AL), Luiza 31 (sick),
    May M. 9, James Y. 6, Marget A. 9/12
    (b. Aug); SELATHILL, Marsh 6 (stepson)
26. JENINO, Carwell (f) 48 (widow) (sick),
    James 23, Mary 19, John 17 (sick),
    Sallie 15 (sick), Martin 12, Martha 9,
    Charlie 8, Franklin 7, Gilbert 3
27. BIRDITT, Samuel 47 (T NC T), Nancy Jane 46,
    John M. 22, Geo. W. 19, Manervea L. 17,
    Ruaward? (f) 14, Eliza J. 12, Martha
    Jane 8

    Page 5, Dist. 4

28. WORTHINGTON, James jr. 50, Hannah 40 (T NC
    T)
29. HAMILTON, John 29, Nancy Jane 26, J. Robert
    6, Leona G. 4, Sarah A. 4/12 (b. Jan)
30. WORTHINGTON, Henry (B) 35, John 6 (son)
    (scarfala--sic), William M. 5, James A.
    4
31. SCHOOLFIELD, P. H. 54 (T VA T), A. B. 55
    (wife) (lame), James C. 19, P. H. jr.
    17 (Lutheran Native Confederacy?)
32. BROWN, J. R. 59 (T NC T), Manervia 50 (wife),
    Nancy C. 26, James R. jr. 22, Thomas C.
    20, John H. 17, W. Franklin 15, Eliza
    Jane 13, Fannie N. 11, I. Hugh 9,
    Robert E. L. 6
33. BROWN, J. C. sr. 24
34. GENTRY, John 65 (epileptic fits), Betsey 57,
    James 24, George 21, Alfred 18, Eliza-
    beth 17
35. SWAFFORD, J. M. 51 (T NC __), Margret 58
    (wife) (lame from fever) (T Ire Ire),
    E. Edwin 23 (miller); MASSY, Jennie 16
    (bond girl); BIRDITT, Harritt 27 (as
    one of family), R. E. 13 (dau); BROWN,
    R. W. (m) 37 (divorced)

    Page 6, Dist. 4

36. SHAHERN?, J. B. 26, Sallie E. 23 (wife),
    Jane 59 (mother) (T VA VA)
37. PATTON, J. A. 44 (carpenter) (lung disease),
    Martha J. 28 (wife), H. E. 7 (son),
    E. W. 6 (son), M. A. 3 (dau); CAVILLE,
    T. C. (f) 12 (no relation)
38. SWAFFORD, Howard 40, Sallie 18; JOHNSON,
    Eva 3 (sis)
39. CLARK, Samuel 25, Sarah 19 (GA GA GA)
40. HENDERSON, T. F. 32, Loudinna? 38 (wife),
    H. Josephine 5, Lenora S. 4, Aury?
    9/12 (b. Feb)
41. CLARK, John A. 28, Permelia 33 (GA GA GA),
    James T. 1, Colwell W. J. 11 (step son)
42. BROWN, C. C. (Mu) 25, Salina 22 (wife),
    Chanie? 52 (mother) (breast complaint),
    Henry 11 (nephew), Emiline 6 (niece);
    HUTCHESON, Malon (B) 2 (nephew)
43. McCLAMEY, R. H. 27 (T NC VA), A. Josie 22
    (wife), Robert 1; ROYTON?, Alice 40
    (mother in law) (broken leg)
44. WORTHINGTON, Jas. 68 (divorced)
45. WORTHINGTON, J. C. (m) 26
46. WORTHINGTON, R. L. 24 (m)
47. WORTHINGTON, Washington (B) 55 (KY T KY),
    Hanah 62, Blle (sic) 6 (g dau), Eliza
    (g dau)

Hh#   Page 7, Dist. 4

48. MONTGOMERY, Jane R. 46 (widow) (sick), Geo.
     P. 19, Ally 17 (dau)
49. HUTCHESON, M. (m) 24, Ursaline 19
50. BIRDITT, Thomas 44, Martha E. 40, R.?
     Franklin 18, Millie 18, George W. 15,
     Sarah 13, Alice 11, Martha 10, Thomas
     H. 6, Havey 2
51. BROWN, Robert (B) 40, Sarah A. 31, Eli 17,
     William 14, Littie 13
52. WORTHINGTON, Fred (B) 28, Narsis 31 (wife),
     Sarah 13, Sidny 6 (son), Lee 4,
     Franklin 2, Thomas 4/12 (Mu) 10/12
     (b. Apr)
53. CARTRIGHT, Henry 34 (hump backed), Jane 24,
     Amanda 10 (dau), Anna 1
54. BROWN, T. O. 45 (school teacher) (injured
     eye) (T VA VA), Mary E. 46 (T VA VA),
     Kittie A. 22 (school teacher), E. E.
     19 (dau), Minnie 15, Thomas C. 14,
     John R. 12, Ida 7, James R. 9
55. WORTHINGTON, R. B. 28 (surveyor)

                 Page 8, Dist. 4

56. SWAFFORD, Alex 29, M. T. 29 (wife), Mary E.
     8, Larkin J. 5, Olie Jane 2, Gather A.
     4/12 (b. Jan)
57. SWAFFORD, Samuel 24, Emiline 19, Thomas H.
     9/12 (b. Sep)
58. HALE, Thomas 37, Jerusha? 32, L. S. 14 (son),
     S. A. 12 (dau), John F. 9, W. A. 6
     (son), Jesse 4
59. HALE, James 35, Texas 25 (wife), Martha J.
     5, William 3, Mary 4/12 (b. Jan)
60. HUTCHESON, W. A. 43, Flora 32 (wife), Josie
     11, Charles 9, Maggie 7; CAFFS?,
     Lizzie 19 (no relation)
61. SMITH, Frank 26, Mary 30, John 8, Martha 6,
     Benjamin 4, Gertrude 3, Leonidus 5/12
     (b. Dec)
62. BROWN, Jas. M. 56 (T NC VA); LEE, T. A. (m)
     26 (no relation); BROWN, James jr. 8
     (nephew), Nancy 45 (sis) (T NC VA),
     Emilie R. 43 (sis) (T NC VA); SMITH,
     Brook 54, D. C. 24 (wife), Elvia 16,
     John H. 14, Brooks jr. 6, Charlie 1

                 Page 9, Dist. 4

63. THURMAN, J. M. 51, Mary E. 51 (wife) (cough),
     Tennessee A. 20, Andy J. 18, Owing 16,
     John H. 12, W. E. 10 (son)
64. McDOWELL, Jane 70 (widow) (T NC NC), Mary
     40 (T T NC), Sarah 28, Isbell 26 (dau)
65. WORTHINGTON, John 22, Nancy J. 22 (T NC T),
     Jesse 8, Anna 6, Lucrecia 4, Ida 1
66. McDOWELL, W. B. 45 (widower) (T NC T), Mar-
     get 26 (dau), James 19 (lame), Nancy
     Jane 14, Thurs 12 (son), Joseph 11,
     Amandy 5 (lame)
67. SMITH, T. F. 38 (T NC T), Zilpha 39 (T KY T),
     William I. 12, James J. 11, Samel Z. 9,
     Mary K. 8, John L. 5, Charles E. 2;
     VANHOY, Andy 18 (stepson) (lame)
68. SMITH, M. J. (f) 62 (heart complaint)
     (widow) (T nC KY), Persillia 28
69. WORTHINGTON, J. C. 49, Mary J. 36, James 18;
     HANKINS, James 1 (g son)

                 Page 10, Dist. 4

70. SMITH, William 20, Martha 18, Nancy Jane
     1-6/12, Wayman 1/12 (b. May)
71. WALKER, George 35 (kidney disease), Mary C.
     30, Susan R. 12, Mary E. 9, J. J. 7
     (dau), Willie D. 5 (lame), E. Franklin
     3
72. WORTHINGTON, David 35, Mary 29
73. FOSTER, William 45, Jane 37, Martin R. 14
     (KY), A. E. 12 (dau) (KY), W. E. 10
     (son) (deformed badly), James A. 7
     (lame), B. Franklin 5, Mary M. 3/12
     (b. Feb)

Hh#   Page 10 (cont'd)

74. WORTHINGTON, Wm. 75, Maria 55, Thomas 22,
     R. J. 21 (son), Evaline 18, Franklin
     jr. 16, Robert 14; McDOWELL, Anna J.
     16 (g dau)
75. BROWN, Sarah 56 (widow), Samuel 34, L. U. 32
     (dau), J. C. 23 (son); WALKER, Rosalea
     20 (no relation); NICKLES, Sallie 90
     (aunt) (SC SC SC)
76. SWAFFORD, S. H. L. 28, M. J. 22 (wife),
     Phineas? J. R. 2, Isaac E. 1
77. BROWN, Thomas 30, Rachel 23, Charlie 4,
     James I. 2

                 Page 11, Dist. 4

78. SEGRAVES, Jesse 37, Angeline 30
79. McDOWELL, W. S. 55 (T PA NC), Kinzy 49
     (bro) (T PA NC), Lucy J. E. 41 (T PA
     NC), James 14 (nephew); MILLER, Sallie
     26 (no relation) (Dept P.M.) (NC NC NC),
     Chalie E. 9/12 (b. Feb) (son) (T T NC)
80. HAWKINS, John 64 (T T NC), Mary E. 38 (wife),
     William 23, Hanah 18, George 14, Lizzie
     12, David 11, Stephie 9, Sallie 6,
     Samuel 7, John 3, Margret 15 (dau in
     law)
81. HALE, John N. 65 (T NC T), Mary A. 65 (T SC
     SC) (lame), Luizy 40
82. HALE, James A. 43 (T T SC)
83. HALE, Elisha 39 (T T SC), Eliabith (sic)
     30, Nancy J. 12, Marandia 10, Isaac 9,
     Rainy 8 (dau), Edna 6, Reckless 4 (son),
     Viola 2
84. HUTCHISON, P. S. 68, Sallie 67 (wife), Mar-
     gret 32, James 11 (g son) (scafula);
     WILSON, Sallie 18 (g dau); HUTCHISON,
     John (B) 21 (no relation--servant),
     S. A. (m) 11 (no relation--servant)

                 Page 12, Dist. 4

85. HUTCHISON, J. T.? 46 (widower), Beckie A.
     18, Virginia 16, Sallie 14
86. HUTCHISON, M. P. jr. 22, Emiline 20 (wife),
     Alison 1 (son)
87. CARTER, Charles 28 (GA GA GA), Annie 27 (GA
     GA GA), Lizzie 9 (GA), Eddie 5 (GA)
88. HUTCHISON, Lucy (B) 46 (GA GA GA), Emiline
     18 (dau) (GA GA GA), Mack 9 (son) (GA
     GA GA)
89. WILSOM?, Matildia 39 (widow) (GA GA GA),
     Willie 20 (son) (GA GA GA)

                 Page 13, Dist. 5

90. POPE, D. S. 34, Mary 28 (wife), Leroy 6
     (CAL), Beatrice 4 (T), Victor 2
91. BILLINGSLEY, J. T. 29, Josie 28 (wife), A.
     E. 3 (son), Lena Rivers 2 (dau)
92. FARMER, W. W. 44 (T GA NC), Viola 39,
     Peniah 17 (teacher), Rhodia 15, Lucindia
     13, Thomas 11, Wade 9, Eliabeth (sic) 7
93. HALE, T. F. 36, S. E. 34 (wife), B. C. 4
     (dau), H. V. 10/12 (b. Aug) (son)
94. HUTCHISON, F. J. 50 (T NC NC), N. A. 48
     (wife), T. A. 18 (son), D. L. 15 (son),
     N. S. 13 (dau), A. C. 10 (son), S. E.
     9 (dau)
95. PAYME, John 25 (GA T T), Eliabeth (sic) 26,
     Eula 1-6/12 (dau) (GA GA T)
96. MUNAHAM, C. 48, Mary 41, M. M. 14 (dau),
     Elender 10 (dau), Edie 7, Nettie 4,
     Josie E. 1 (dau)
97. BOYD, S. W. 63 (VA VA VA), Susan 61, Byron
     42, Carline 32

                 Page 14, Dist. 5

98. HALE, Sallie 65 (widower), Emiline 32,
     Susan 25, Begiman 27
99. HALE, John 56 (fever) (T NC NC), Mary A.
     56 (T VA VA), Joesph (sic) 18, Isaac R.
     16, James 14 (broken arm), B. V. 13
     (dau)

Hh#   Page 14 (cont'd)

100. HALE, Martin 27 (has fits), Mary 25,
       Margret 7, S. W. 5 (son)

               Page 15, Dist. 5

101. HALE, Thomas 69 (T SC NC), Z. V. 67 (wife)
       (NC NC NC)
102. HALE, S. S. 32 (T T NC), A. E. 30 (wife),
       W. P. 6 (son), Ollie V. 8/12 (b. Sep)
       (dau); OWINGS, Lu (f) 44 (cousin)
103. HALE, W. C. 37, Nancy A. 37 (wife), Mary J.
       16, W. T. 15 (son), J. F. 13 (son),
       C. A. 10 (dau), Jesse 7, Emmitt 3,
       Emma 3, A. A. 2/12 (b. Apr) (dau)
104. SWAFFORD, J. D. 49 (T SC SC), Elizabeth 47
       (T NC KY), Nancy J. 21, Mary 17, Sarah
       E. 15, James 12, Aaron 10; McCLAMY,
       M. A. 22 (relationship omitted), John
       4 (son)
105. HINES, John 70, Mary E. 21 (wife), Crawford
       2; McPHERSON, M. 14 (sis in law)
106. SHOEMATE, Wm. 75, Fannie 64
107. CLAYTON, Nancy 57
108. WALKER, E. 35 (f), John 17, Luesie 12,
       William 6, James 5
109. HAMPILTON, Mary 79 (widow) (SC SC SC),
       Delia 64 (dau?) (T SC SC)

               Page 16, Dist. 5

110. OWINGS, W. M. 48, Sarah A. 44 (wife),
       William 21, Leusie A. 18, Tho. J. 15,
       Z. E. 12 (dau), M. F. 10 (son), R.
       Jackson 8, Sarah A. 4; HUSER, S. H.
       1 (nephew)
111. CLARK, John? 20, Amandy 22, Malcolm 6/12 (b.
       Nov) (son)
112. LOYD, Henry (Mu) 25, Evaline 25, J. Osker
       5, Nancy 3, Martha J. 1
113. WILSON, Joseph (Mu) 20, Martha Jane 21,
       Isibell 4, Mary 2
114. SIMMONS, A. J. 39, M. L. 34 (wife), Arbelle
       11
115. SIMMONS, F. 20, Martha J. 17 (wife), Lida-
       belle 1 (dau)
116. SIMMONS, J. P. 37, Nancy J. 37 (wife), Mary
       L. 13, John A. 10, Susan J. 8, L. A. 6
       (dau), B. P. 4 (dau), Maud M. 2
117. BILLINGSLEY, A. B. 66, Susan J. 52 (wife),
       Thomas S. 21, Dora 15, Tecora? 13

               Page 15, Dist. 5
               (should be 17)

118. HOGE, Nathaniel 32, E. A. 30 (wife), Sarah
       8, E. E. 7 (son), Nancy J. 4
119. BILLINGSLEY, Nute (Mu) 50, Mahalia 26, John
       11, Sarah E. 10, Hatense 7 (dau), Rick
       5, Rosa Lee 2, Adel 9/12 (b. Nov)
       (dau)
120. RANKIN, Alfred (B) 33, Mary (Mu) 28, James
       H. (B) 13 (lame), Rella 10, Florance
       (Mu) 8 (niece)
121. BILLINGSLEY, Ach (B) 68, Luizy (Mu) 42
       (wife)
122. FAMER, Samuel 36, Martha 21 (wife), Ida 1
123. CLARK, W. B. 55, Mary 49 (wife)
124. DYRE, Will 38, Sarah 40, Martha 72 (mother
       in law); WOODS, S. A. 18 (f) (no re-
       lation)
125. COX, J. M. 47, Mary 44 (wife), Nancy A. 23,
       Chalie 21 (son), R. C. 18 (son),
       James 16, Mary Jane 13, Malindia 12,
       Sarah 8, Maudia 6, Ida 2

               Page 18, Dist. 5

126. ERWIN, Harvy 52, Mary 24 (CT CT CT), Ada 7
       (T T T), Rufus 5, Willie 3
127. BROCK, Wm. (Mu) 60, Mary A. (W) 29 (wife),
       Burd (Mu) 20, D. C. 18 (son), Emma 16,
       Eliza Jane 12, Willie 5, Crosha 5
       (dau), Statira 2, Ida Jane 4/12 (b.
       Feb)
128. SMITH, Wm. 17, Lillie 20, Cathern 3

Hh#   Page 18 (cont'd)

129. ATCHLEY, James 25, Lu 21 (wife), Samuel 3,
       Jane 2
130. RANDALS, T. A. 34 (MS KY AL), S. A. 34
       (wife), Benjamin 8
131. JORDAN, W. A. 36 (T SC T), Sarah 42 (T VA
       VA), Nannie 10; JOHNSON, Margret 30
       (sis in law) (T VA VA), Jarott 12 (son)
       (T VA VA)

               Page 19, Dist. 5

132. JOHNSON, P. C. 26 (SC SC SC), Mary 26,
       Sarah 5, S. E. 3 (son), W. C. 1 (son)
133. BORING, J. H. 60 (blacksmith) (VA VA T),
       Abgail 49 (wife) (T VA VA), W. M. 14
       (son), Mary E. 11, Rosa C. 9
134. BORING, P. H. 19 (married within yr--Dec),
       Matildia 20 (wife)
135. BORING, J. D. 18 (married within yr--Apr),
       Eliabeth 16 (wife)
136. WORTHINGTON, L. (B) 30 (cabinet maker),
       Mary (Mu) 22 (wife), Boyd (B) 5, Elmo
       4, Ezear (Mu) 2 (dau), J. N. 8/12 (b.
       Jan) (son)
137. BILLINGSLEY, Anderson (B) 48, Malindia 46,
       Nathan 16, John 10, Emmitt 7, Sarildia
       5, Haston 3, Alfred 9/12 (b. Sep),
       Lucus 25 (son) (lame)
138. BILLINGSLEY, Martin (B) 45, Emilise (Mu)
       36, Wisly? (B) 10 (no relation),
       Etta 3 (g dau), Emilin 17 (no relation)
139. MERCER, Peter 46 (T VA NC), Bitha 38 (T VA
       T), Mary A. 23, James D. 19, Sarah 15,
       Harrison 13, Ferester 11, Clementine 9,
       Jane 7, Floyd 6, Eli 4

               Page 20, Dist. 5

140. COFFMAN, M. 23 (GA T GA), Fannie 27 (wife),
       Lula 5, Ada A. 4, Mary M. 2, Annie 5/12
       (b. Oct)
141. POLLARD, I. N. 43, Martha J. 37 (wife),
       Sallie 13, James 12, Charlie 8, Kittie
       5, Julie 2
142. GILL, Samuel P. 27, Endie 23, Rhoda E. 6,
       Samuel F. 5, George W. 2, Robert A.
       3/12 (b. Mar)
143. BILLINGSLEY, L. T. 37 (T VA T), Mary E. 31
       (wife), Samuel W. 5, Flora Jane 3,
       John M. 8/12 (b. Nov)
144. BILLINGSLEY, Jane R. 66 (widow) (T Holland
       Holland)
145. SMITH, James (Mu) 22, Jeonoka? (B) 20
       (wife), Callie (Mu) 4/12 (b. Oct)
146. JONES, L. W. 57 (widow), R. P. 25 (son),
       L. C. (son) 23, G. C. 20 (son), L. A.
       17 (dau), James N. 10
147. STEPHENS, Moor 41, Arbyjane 36, J. B. 15
       (son), T. A. 13 (dau), Flora E. 10,
       Mary M. 7, Martha L. 4, James M. 8/12
       (b. Sep)

               Page 21, Dist. 5

148. ACUFF, J. S. 38, Nancy Jane 33 (wife), J. D.
       14 (son), W. L. 12 (son), E. F. 9 (son),
       M. A. 6 (dau) (TX), C. E. 3 (dau) (T),
       John E. 1/12 (b. May); SPEARMAN, Violet
       (B) 17 (servant)
149. CUNNINGHAM, C. O. 30 (T VA VA), Mary 23
       (wife) (MO T T), G. B. 2 (son), J. E. 1
       (dau)
150. HALL, Jacob 26, Armeula? 23, J. B. 5 (son),
       J. E. 2 (son)
151. PAYNE, N. P. 34 (f), N. B. 22 (stepson),
       Mary L. 15, A. T. 11 (son), H. P. 2/12
       (b. Apr) (son)
152. HUTCHESON, R. B. 40, Roena 28 (wife);
       ROMINES, Henry 12 (no relation)
153. McCLAMEY, Jas. 30, Virginia 30, Mary E.
       7/12 (b. Nov)

Hh#	Page 22, Dist. 5

154. WORTHINGTON, Martin 29, Czear (sic) 30 (wife)
155. SEGRAVES, Mary 59 (widow), F. S. A. 29 (dau), Hester A. 20, Nancy 18, Willie K. 14, Brown 44 (step dau)
156. SEGRAVES, J. F. R. 26, Sarah E. 24 (wife)
157. RANKIN, D. F. 29, E. E. 19 (wife), Ada B. 9/12 (b. Oct)
158. RANKIN, Dovie? (f) 41; MITCHELL, Lue 15 (niece), Sallie 11 (niece)
159. HUTCHESON, Reuben (B) 50, Charlote 32 (wife), W. H. 14 (son), L. E. 11 (dau), Jeffison 9
160. LAWSON, J. A. 37, Martha E. 34, F. M. 17 (son), A. E. 14 (son), Mary 8, P. A. 5 (dau), Jas. M. 1
161. GENTRY, J. P. 35, Mary 25 (wife), Leroy 8, A. S. J. 6 (son), Anna J. 4, F. H. 1 (son), Sallie 78 (mother)
162. PATTON, Owings 50 (miller), Mary 44, Elija 18, Emlie? 15, Nancy 13, Mattie 10, Lizzie 7, Nyott 6 (son), William 3

Page 23, Dist. 5

163. PENDERGRASS, A. 28, Sarah C. 20, M. L. 2/12 (b. Apr) (m)
164. SIMMONS, Jas. T. 48, Nancy Jane 47, A. F. 18 (son), Sarah Jane 17, B. S. 14 (son), W. E. 12 (son), Mary Jackson 7
165. PENDERGRASS, Wamey? 55 (blacksmith), Beckie 49 (wife), M. M. 24 (son), Arbzeim 21 (wife)
166. HENDERSON, Anne 51 (widow), W. R. 20 (son)
167. SWAFFORD, C. 23 (widow), Ha 16 (son), Lu 14 (dau), Nason 8
168. ACUFF, J. H. 35, Mary T. 23 (wife), William 11/12 (b. Jul), Millican (surname?) 20 (sis in law)
169. ATCHLEY, G. W. 54, Lucindia 50 (wife), Mary T. 22, Samuel 19, L. Florence 12, Thomas A. 9, Margret Jane 6
170. ATCHLEY, J. W. M. 25, E. L. 21 (wife), Samuel R. 3, L. Jane 1
171. HOLT, Thomas 55, Amanda 43, E. T. 11 (dau), E. A. 10 (dau), S. L. 3 (son)

Page 24, Dist. 5

172. DOTSON, Jack 54, Belle 30 (wife); YATES, Mary 18 (dau), Thomas 25 (son in law) (one leg off); DOTSON, Thos. 15 (son), John 10, Elleur 11 (dau), Sallie 9, Jessie 6, Martha 3, Mindia 1-1/2 (dau), Calhoun 8/12 (b. Jan)
173. NEDD, Samuel (Mu) 24, Amandia (B) 20, Thursday 3 (dau)
174. RICHARDS, Smith 23, Julia 20 (WI T MA); IVES?, John 26 (no relation) (works at sawmill) (MD ___ ___)
175. LOWERY, M. (B) 35 (m), Andy 18 (son), Bird 9, Sarah Jane 5, Charlie 3, James L. (Mu) 1
176. MOLES?, Henry 50, Hanah 45, Elizabeth 22 (these two names crossed out), Robert A. 7, Henry 5, Elbert Lee 1; BROWN, L. (m) 50 (no relation), Mary E. 16 (no relation), B. J. (f) 13 (no relation), B. J. (f) 45 (no relation), Mary 75 (no relation)

Page 25, Dist. 5

177. NORTHRUP, S. J. 26 (T NY NY), Ellen 24 (wife), Adabelle 3, Lela 1
178. FARMER, Martin 39, Syvester 28 (wife), Lewis 16, Amanda 12, William 11, Jerusha 8, Samuel 6, Martha A. 4, James Ross 1
179. CURTIS, Levander 28, Manervia 26, Ada 10 (dau), Lewis 7, Granville 5, Martin 1
180. GENTRY, Robert 26 (blacksmith), Trasher? 25 (wife), Howel C. 3
181. CURTIS, H. 22, Nancy 20 (wife), Mary Jane 8/12 (b. Oct); MASSEY, James 18 (son in law)

Hh#	Page 25 (cont'd)

182. COX, Marion 35, Alice 22 (wife), Emma 4, Charlie 3, Early 1
183. SWAFFORD, Aaron sr. 67, Maria 59, Thos. L. 24, Calhon 22, Pardittier 19 (dau)
184. SWAFFORD, Matt (B) 55, Jane 40 (wife), Charlie 23, Richard 22, Thomas J. 20, Lewis 18, James 13, Aaron 10, Slyman 8 (son), George 6, Mary M. 1

Page 26, Dist. 5

185. CLARK, Daniel 65, Anna 35 (wife), Richard 12, Mary 10, James 8, Jacob 6, Perdittia 4, TAylor 1
186. COFFMAN, T. J. 52, Martha A. E. 42 (wife) (GA GA SC), J. C. 13 (T T GA), Jas. C. 10, Mountville 7, T. C. 1
187. PANKEY, Charles (B) 52, Lucindia 53, George 27
188. BILLBERY, Henry 28, Mary 25, Lonzo 6, Darious 3, M. Jane 1
189. BILLBERY, Chamberlain 53, Persilia 50, Doe 23 (son), Carter 18, Matildia 16, William 15 (lame), Isaac 13, Jermiah 10
190. PATTON, F. T. 22, L. C. 22 (wife), O. A. 2 (son), H. E. 2/12 (b. Mar) (son)
191. NIDD, Jane (Mu) 63 (widow), Anne 20, Lewis 18
192. HUTCHESON, Cas. (Mu) 25 (widow), Edith May 1

Page 27, Dist. 10

193. BRIDGMAN, Alex (Mu) 35, Amada 36 (wife), John Henry 12, Lula 10, Rush 8, James 6, Arnold 3
194. HUTCHESON, Lee 26
195. PANKEY, Mary 51 (widow) (T KY T), Samuel S. 32, James S. 30; STONRY, Matildia 42 (sis) (T KY T); MONTGOMERY, K. B. 32 (cousin--m) (T T GA)
196. SWAFFORD, Green (B) 37, Lishie 47 (wife), John 7, William 6, Sarah 21, Amandia 19, Harriott (Mu) 5, Isaac (B) 4, Harmon 3
197. CHILDS, John T. 30 (SC SC SC), Jane 28, Mary C. 9, John H. 7, William M. 5, L. Susan 3, Eliza Jane 1
198. MULINEX, W. O. 32, Margret E. 26 (wife), Nannie C. 6, Sarah Jane 4

Page 28, Dist. 10

199. KING, Jon. H. 46 (T NC VA), Nancy 41 (T VA VA), Joel? N. 19 (lame), W. R. 18, Robert F. 16, Margret T. 14, Mary E. 10, Charlie 8, Sallie 6
200. DYRE, James 38, Edie 29, Larance 14
201. THURMAN, C. 24, S. Jane 22 (wife), Laura 11/12 (b. May)
202. THURMAN, Wm. 56, Melatia 48, Mary Jane 23, Dorthula 21, William 14
203. THURMAN, Anderson 31, Rachel L. 30 (could), Bettie Jane 8, Melitia L. 6, Margret A. 2; HENDERSON, Mary 23 (cousin) (divorced), John E. 4 (son)
204. THOMAS, Jas. 47, Mary 49 (could), Samuel J. 21, J. M. 18 (son), W. A. 15 (son), Elizabeth 13
205. THURMAN, Henry 25, Amanda 21, Lillie 1
206. NEAL, M. C. 34, R. A. 30 (wife), Susan E. 13, Mary Ann 10, Martha A. 8, John Z. 6, Sarah B. 3, Emma Jane 2, Jas. H. 7/12 (b. Jan); LAW, Delania 70 (no relation) (NC NC VA)

Page 29, Dist. 10

208. SEGRAVES, Ben 42 (club footed), Lottie 35, William 18, John 12, Eliza 11, James 9, Cathern 7, Charlie 5, Hester Anna 3, Susan 1
209. THURMAN, Saml. 30, Sarah E. 27, William A. 9, Rebecka C. 7, Jas. D. 6, Sarah A. 2, C. Wilson 1
210. WRIGHT, Thos. 45, Mary 36, Mary 17, Sarah 13, Martha 12, James 8, Minnie F. 6, Samuel 1, John 18 (son), Mary M. 20

Hh#	Page 29 (cont'd)

211. McDONOLD, John 38, Margret 34, Mary 16, James 14, Ella 12, Greenbery 10, Jan 8, Robert 6, Thomas 2
212. ROBERTS, Jas. L. 22, Martha A. 20, Susan C. 3, Jas. H. 1/12 (b. May)

Page 30, Dist. 10

213. DUN, Susan 57 (widow), Mary 25, John W. 22, Henry B. 18, Susan C. 9 (g dau), Jas. H. 5 (g son)
214. SWAFFORD, Rufus 26, Matildia 21, T. Alfred 3, Mary Jane 1
215. ETHERTON, John 65 (stealing), Matildia 64, William 23, James W. 19, Elizabeth 17, Harrit J. 16, John 14
216. MATHIS, Leander 44, Tennessee 39, John A. J. 17, Martha C. 15, Thomas 13, James 11, Samuel 9, Daniel M. 6
217. JORDAN, Emma 33, Bettie 13, Nancy 6, John 1
218. SWAFFORD, L. 24 (widow), Sarah E. 7 (fever), Sephronie 5, Enie 3 (son), Willie C. 1
219. GIDDEON, Beckie 31 (widow) (NC SC SC), W. Jackson 13 (T T NC), George W. 11, Mary Jane 7, Jasper 4, Sallie 2
220. WEBB, Jane 26 (widow), Frances 8, James A. 4, George W. 2

Page 31, Dist. 10

221. HALE, W. H. 39, Nancy 36; BROWN, Lucy 25 (no relation) (servant), Martha 2 (dau)
222. SWAFFORD, Jeferson 60, Martha 50, John 12, DYRE, Sintha 22 (dau), John M. 3 (son)
223. MILLS, Levi 47 (GA GA GA), Hettie 42 (GA GA GA), Orphis 20 (GA), Sefforie 18 (GA), Carline 12 (T), Maryland 10 (dau), Herritt 8, Evaline 7, Kittie 4, Chester 11/12 (b. Jul), Martha 69 (mother) (cripled) (GA GA GA), Syntha 27 (sis) (GA GA GA)
224. MILLS, F. J. 37 (GA GA GA), L. H. 30 (wife) (T T KY), M. L. 7 (dau), J. A. W. 5 (son), O. J. 4 (dau), Ida M. 2, Jas. E. 7/12 (b. Jan)
225. ROLANDS, Elvira 45 (widow) (T GA T), M. E. 24 (dau) (T GA T), W. ?. 21 (son), B. A. 12 (dau), Samuel 6, Jacob 2
226. RICHEY, H. A. 57, Thursy 54 (wife) (AL AL AL), Robert 22, Nancy J. 18, Mary A. 13
227. RICHEY, James 27, A. S. 20 (wife)
228. MITTS, Andy 50, Eliza Jane 44, J. R. 24 (son), Samuel 20, William 16, Rhoda 13, M. A. 5 (dau); WHITE, Rusel 70 (father in law), Susan S. 60 (mother in law)
229. MITTS, Nancy 55 (T T VA), Stephen 19 (son), William 40 (bro) (T T T)

Page 32, Dist. 10

230. HENDERSON, R. M. 47, Mary L. 37 (wife), Alvin 18, Sarah C. 15, Luesie 13, R. M. 11 (son), Jackson 9, Syntha 5, Beckie W. 3, Amanda C. 1/12 (b. May)
231. ROSE, J. A. 40, L. J. 39 (wife), Mary I. 19; WYERICK, J. A. 8 (m) (no relation); HUSE, Elizabeth 75 (mother in law)
232. SHAW, Joseph 72, Mary A. 60 (wife), Sarah C. 16 (dau) (fever)
233. HENDERSON, Jasper 37, Harrit E. 29, G. Henry 12, Thos. E. 9, Sarah 8, Sampson J. 7, John 4, Flora 2, V. I. 1/12 (b. May)
234. HENDERSON, Jas. 87, Elizabeth 73 (wife)
235. HENDERSON, Frank (½ idiotic) 44, Sarah N. 48, Mary E. 6
236. BROWN, Elisha 44 (blacksmith), Sarah 25 (wife), Jessee C. 13, Rohda A. 7, James 6, Reuben 5, Churchfield A. 8/12 (b. Sep)

Hh#	Page 33, Dist. 10

237. MILLAKIN, Calvin 50, Sarah 52, Emilin 28, Pery 23, Eliza Jane 16, Victoria 12
238. MILLAKIN, P. P. 23, Amanda J. 25 (wife), Lee Ann 1
239. HENDERSON, Bird 40, Rebecka A. 40, Martha J. 20, Mary Ann 17, Jas. R. 10, Marilda 7, H. V. 5 (dau), G. Thos. 1-10/12
240. GILL, John 40, Martha 35, Samuel W. 11, Savanah E. 9, John A. 4, Amanda E. 3, Andy 1/12 (b. May)
241. McKINNIE, John 29, Nancy 49 (wife)
242. MILLER, Eliza 37 (widower) (breaking?), Thomas 16, William 12, Larance 8, Mary 6
243. WORTHINGTON, Wm. 38, Margret 29, Franklin 8, Forest 6, Robert 3, James 2
244. PENDERGRASS, Nancy 51 (widow), L. N. 20 (son)
245. PEARCE, Rachel 50 (widow), A. M. 28 (son) (loafer), J. R. 18, Martha J. 7 (g dau), Charlie 5 (g son); CLARK, J. J. 54 (relationship omitted), Nancy 39; JOHNSON, C. 8 (no relation) (m)

Page 34, Dist. 10

246. GEARY, Hannah 55 (SC SC SC), Carline 46 (sis) (SC SC SC); JOHNSON, Eliza 20 (niece) (SC SC SC), Jackson 16 (nefew) (SC SC SC), Crocket 15 (nefew) (SC SC SC), James 10 (nefew) (SC SC SC)

Page 1, Pikeville

1. NORWOOD, St. Clair 58 (T MD T), Catharine 58 (T NC T), Fanny 21, Henry B. 25 (blacksmith), Mary E. 22 (son's wife)
2. HALE, Jeremiah 70 (physician) (VA NC NC), Nancey 76 (VA VA VA), Ewin 12 (stepson) (T T VA); AGEE, Nicholas 35 (son in law) (house carpenter), Martha 36 (dau) (opium eating) (crippled) (VA), Victorine 8 (g dau) (T T VA), Margarett 6 (g dau) (T T VA), Hortense 4 (g dau) (T T VA), Nancey 2 (g dau) (T T VA)
4. LANE, Gantt 35 (merchant), Lucey 28; LEA, Elizabeth 14 (Mu) (servant)
5. THOMAS, William 53 (merchant) (Eng Eng Eng), Grace 44 (Canada Scot Ire), William 23 (Can) (clerk in store), Harry 21 (clerk in store) (IA), Freddy 18 (IA), Katie 16 (IA), Rosa 14 (IA), Laveno 11 (IA), Sarah 8 (T), Forester 7/12 (b. Nov); KEELER, Sarah 65 (mother in law) (old age--crippled) (Ire Ire Ire)
6. BARNETT, James 38? (physician), Gertrude 20 (wife), Mable 3, Herman 1; RANKEN, Amanda 40 (mother in law)
7. FURGERSON, Samuel 45 (hotel keeper), Amey 32 (wife) (NY CT CT), Ada 3; ESSEX, Elizabeth 20 (servant) (T NC T); WITTEN?, E. O. (f) 43 (widow) (teacher) (VA ME VA) (boarder), Sada 16 (boarder) (VA VA VA); MERSER, Forester 32 (boarder--lawyer) (T KY T), Mary 20 (boarder--teacher) (VA VA VA), HOWARD, John 45 (boarder) (clerk of court); GILBERT, Jessey 38 (boarder-scaler) (T PA PA); THOMPSON, James 19 (T NC T) (boarder); WORTHINGTON, Reuben 30 (boarder) (county surveyor)

Page 2, Pikeville

8. CARR, Daniel 42 (minister) (VA VA VA), Sarah 38 (VA VA VA), Nancy 17 (VA), Samuel 14 (VA), Mary 12 (VA), Sallie 8 (VA)
9. BOYD?, William 40 (blacksmith), Nancey 37, Sallie 10
10. FRANKLIN, Peter 63 (shoe maker) (VA VA VA), Esther 42 (wife) (NC NC NC), Anna 9 (step dau) (IN IN NC)
11. MOZEN?, Robert A. 36 (dentist) (T T NC), Martha 39, Walter 7, Lilla 4; KNIGHT, Margaret 35 (servant) (NC NC NC)

Hh#	Page 2 (cont'd)

12. DUGGER, Terressa 40 (widow), Violett 18
13. BRIDGMAN, Neoma 37 (widow) (T NC NC)
14. BRIDGMAN, Don 25, Mary 25, Ader 5 (dau), Malen 3 (dau), James 4/12 (b. Nov)
15. BARBER, Edward 61 (wagon maker) (Eng Eng Eng), Ina 43 (wife) (VT VT VT), Helen 20 (teacher) (IL), Edward 19 (IL, George 17 (IL), Frank 12 (IN), Ina 10 (IN)
16. ABLE, William 32 (shoe maker), Letha 25 (T VA VA), Loftus 6, William 5, Martha 2, James 7/12 (b. Oct)
17. BROWN, Carter (Mu) 24, Cintha 18
18. THOMPSON, Sarah 40 (widow), William 15, Jerry 13, ANNIS, John 28 (boarder-- mail carrier); JONES, William 15 (boarder--mail carrier)
19. PANTER (PARKER?), Mary 72 (hotel keeper (old age) (VA VA VA), Sarah 43 (dau) (T VA VA); TULLOSO, James A. 70 (boarder--retired merchant) (VA VA VA); ROBERSON, Inda (B) 20 (servant)

Page 3, Pikeville

20. PANTER, Sampson 37 (T NC VA), Mary 30 (dau in law) (NC NC NC); ROBERSON, Tole? (B) 22 (laborer)
21. SULLASS, John (B) 30, Rebecca 24, William 6, Ross 3, Charles 1
22. BROWN, William A. 34 (merchant), Mary 30 Lizza 12, Luther 8, Luler 4 (dau); GREER, Martha (Mu) 28 (servant)
23. ROSS, James A. 43 (physician), Jane 40, Sidney 9 (son), Flora 7, Charles 8/12 (b. Sep); LOCK, Maybell 15 (niece)
24. HART, Henry W. 43 (CT CT CT), Eller 35 (wife) (PA PA PA), Hattia 7, Etter 5 (dau), Nella 1; FLINN, Mary 20 (servant); BORING, John 27 (boarder-- blacksmith); HENRY, Frank 27 (boarder --merchant) (PA PA PA); McJUNKINS, James 22 (laborer)
25. MOZEN, John C. 31 (lawyer), Susan 25, Flora 4, Virginia 1, Olla 1 (dau)
26. HALE, John P. 38 (jailor) (VA VA VA), Nancey 35, Virginia 18, Isaac 14, Joseph 12, John 9, Hallie 7, Mary 4; STEPHENS, Jack (prisoner) (AR AR AR); BRANNON, Damon 24 (prisoner)

Page 4, Dist. 6

27. HENRY, Alfred 32 (PA PA PA), Caroline 28 (sis) (PA PA PA); COMLEY, Etta 21 (servant) (WI __ __)
28. HALL, Jessey 42 (grocer), Hixey 41, Henry 18 (clerk in store), Laura 16, Mar- shall 14, Austin 9
29. BRIDGMAN, Alex (B) 35 (VA VA VA), Amanda 35, John 12, Lula 9, Rush 8, James 7, Arnold 6
30. BROWN, Jackson (B) 35 (T T VA), Sarah 48 (wife) (VA VA VA)
31. JONES, Thomas 45 (physician) (SC SC SC), Lora 37 (GA NC GA), Detie 13 (GA), M____ 10 (dau) (SC), Joshua 8 (T), Kettey 5, Lora 2
32. SPEARS, Peter (B) 67 (crippled) (VA VA VA), Comfrey 40 (wife) (GA GA GA), Clarey 15 (dau) (T T T), Caroline 14, Adaline 10, Charles 8
33. GREER, Cilley (B) 27, Clarey 15 (wife), Martha 4 (dau), Edward 4/12 (b. Nov)
34. REESE, Dock 31, Sarah 34, David 4, Minnie 3, James 10/12 (b. Jun); KNIGHT, Martha 16 (step dau), Laura 12 (step dau), Florence 11 (step dau), Nancy 65 (step mother) (pentioner) (crippled)
35. ROBERSON, Hezekiah 38, Esther 24 (wife), James 5, Lenie 2 (dau), Sallie 9/12 (b. Aug); MOORE, Sallie 16 (servant); LARRENCE, Whittenburg 13 (boarder); HALL, Eliza 50 (boarder), Eva 22 (boarder)

Hh#	Page 5, Dist. 6

36. ACUFF, William 61 (widower) (T VA T), Mary 29, John 27, Joseph 25, Jane 21, William 17; SWAFFORD, Thomas 18 (laborer); BRIDGMAN, John (B) 11 (laborer)
37. BOYD, John L. 26, Martha 30, Effa 4 (worms), Emma 2
38. BOYD, Lafayette 30, Rebecca 31, Erasmus 10, Halley 5
39. PANKY, Calvin (B) 53 (rheumatism), Lucinda 50, George 17, John 14, William 12, Samuel 10, Netta 11, Lucinda 9, Budie 5 (son), Mary 4, James 25 (son), Ellen 20 (dau in law), Rogers 2 (g son)
40. HENSON, Samuel 36, Martha 25, Kittura 7, Mary 2
41. RIGSBEY, Gleam? 43, Nancy 38 (wife), Samuel 10, Alonzo 5, Rachiel 4, Samuel 1
42. SWOFFORD, Jane 18 (step dau) (this entry may belong with household 41 above)
43. (County Poor House) HEARD, John 59 (shoemaker) (Eng Eng Eng), Elizabeth 40 (wife), Sophia 5, Adda 4, Rose 2, Lilla 2; WHITTENBURG, Susan 73 (mother in law); CHRISTIAN, Christopher 80 (pauper) (old age--crippled) (Den Den Den); SIMMONS, John 65 (pauper) (idiotic--crippled); SWAFFORD, Samuel 35 (pauper) (epolepsy--insane--crippled); LEWIS, Dalton 20 (pauper) (idiotic-- crippled); CURTIS, Cathorine 38 (pauper) (palsey--crippled); FURGERSON, Elizabeth 21 (pauper) (cronic mutretus--crippled)

Page 6, Dist. 6

44. BAIN, John 60 (T NC T), Sarah 52, Susan 27 (chills--fever), Sarah 21 (chills-- fever), Thomas 16 (chills--fever), Mary 14, Matilda 12, Josephine 10, Caledonia 7
45. ELLERSON, Melvina 58 (widow), Francis 26, James 23, Margarett 20, David 12, Ider 10 (dau), Eller 8 (dau)
46. CARD, Bird 46 (T VA T), Sarah 41, Lucinda 20, Tennessee 18, Alta 15, James 14, Etta 13, Sarah 9, Jennetta 8, Milas 5, infant (m) 3/12
47. VERNON, Caswell 50 (T NC NC), Alexander 48 (bro) (T NC NC), Octavo 46 (sis) (T NC NC), Nancy 40 (sis) (T NC NC), Sarah (B) 16 (servant); RIGSBEY, John 23 (laborer)
48. GREER, Henry C. 41 (T VA Ire), Hortense 38, Arthusa 18, Wetherton 16, James 14, Moses 12, Dion 10, Elizabeth 8, Emila 6, Sylvester 4, Lucinda 2; SULLIVAN, Buck 17 (laborer)

Page 7, Dist. 6

49. AGEE, Samuel 59 (cabinett workman) (T VA VA), Dorthela 37, Samul 22 (works in black- smith shop), Lanora 20, Irena 14, Reck 17 (son); WHITTENBURG, Marla 5 (step dau) (T Eng T), Jane 5 (step dau) (T Eng T)
50. TULLOSS, Johnathan (B) 44, Jane 42, Mary 13, Charley 8, Della 6, James 3, Mixey 3/12 (son)
51. LOYD, Charles (B) 40 (T T KY)
52. BARBER, William 22 (IL VT Eng), Bersha 23 (wife), James 1
53. BEACH, Mary 29 (divorced), Luther 11, Allice 5, Jinney 3/12 (dau)
54. BRIDGMAN, Jack (Mu) 38, Harrit 35, Allestra 11, William 7, James 4, Bird 2; COLBERT, Carroll 7 (nephew), Sarah (B) 16 (niece)
55. McJUNKENS, Jack 52 (mill right) (T SC VA), Lucinda 49, Susan 24, Danil 16, Samuel 14, Babe 10 (son), Sanna 8 (dau)
56. WHITTENBURG, Isaac 64, Marilda 54 (wife) (T VA VA), John 17, Amanda 13
57. ROBERSON, James 44 (lawyer), Penelope 33, Isaac 10, Laurence 9, Ada 7, James 5, Spears 4, Samuel 2, William 1

BLEDSOE COUNTY

Hh#   Page 8, Dist. 6

58. KELLEY, James 36, Euphema 23 (wife), John 7,
    Richard 6, William 3, infant 4/30
    (dau); SMITH, Julia 20 (servant);
59. SPRING, Thomas (Mu) 55, Sarah 53, Volentine
    14 (son) (dispepsia--crippled), Lafay-
    ette 16, George 12 (g son), John 6 (g
    son)
60. RIGSBEY, Lucinda 65 (widow), Martha 28,
    Lucinda 27 (seamstress) (crippled--
    white swelling), Frances 26, George
    25; SWOPE, James 15 (g son), George
    10 (g son)
61. ANDERSON, James 25, Nancy 25, Aaron 12 (son),
    David 5, infant 2 (son)
62. McREYNOLDS, Johnsey (B) 57 (blacksmith),
    Cela 40 (wife), Brown 17 (crippled by
    white swelling), Lucinda 14, Sarah 8,
    Mary 6, Isa 1; BRIDGMAN, George 44
    (boarder) (VA VA VA)
63. CUMMINGS, Rosa (Mu) 46 (widow), Thomas 21,
    Harrison 19 (wound in head), William
    16, Vann 12
64. HENRY, Milton 22 (Mu), Cintha 18, Oliver 1;
    SPRING, Lucinda (B) 60 (relationship
    omitted)

                    Page 9, Dist. 6

65. HENSON, Erastus 25, Christena 30 (sis);
    SKELLEM, Ida 7 (niece); BROWDER, Alex
    (B) 17 (laborer)
66. HENSON, William 38, Mary 39, Kittura 12,
    Johnathan 8, Perditta 7
67. ROBERSON, Reuben (B) 38 (T T GA), Angeline
    33, Maranda 16, Charles 8/12
68. SCHOOLFIELD, William 60, Mary 54, Robert 30
    (lawyer), Virginia 23, Floyd 21,
    William 17
69. BRIDGMAN, Essix (B) 30, Mary 23, Alexander
    9 (son), Adda 5, Lawrence 3
70. McREYNOLDS, Samul (B) 23, Sarah 22 (billious
    fever--crippled), William 4/12
71. STEPHENS, William 76 (T VA NY), Martha 66,
    Samul 27; FRADA, Elizabeth 18 (servant)
72. MITCHELL, Gibs (B) 45 (T VA VA), Mary 45 (VA
    VA VA), Mary 14 (T VA VA), Katy 10 (T
    VA VA), Milly 8 (T VA VA), John 2 (T
    VA VA), Violett 16 (T VA VA)
73. STEPHENS, Isaac 45, Margarett 38
74. TUCKER, Moses 58 (NC NC NC), Martha 51,
    Melvina 34 (dau), Emaline 28 (St.
    Vitus dance--crippled), Mary 24, James
    23, Eliza 19, John 17, Rachiel 14,
    Christiana 11

                    Page 10, Dist. 6

75. WYOTT, John 22, Nancy 21, Amanda 5 (dau),
    Flora 3
76. BROCK, Elihu 53 (crippled--gravel) (AL T T),
    Margaret 49 (KY T T), Horace 19,
    Roxany 16, Amanda 14, Alvis 13
77. BROWN, Elijah 42 (T VA VA), Lotta 27 (wife)
    (NY NY NY), William 11, May 9, Berta
    4, Lucy 1; BROWN, Sarah 82 (mother)
    (VA VA VA)
78. NORTHRUP, Solyman 48 (lawyer) (CT CT CT),
    Nancy 40, William (Mu) 13 (servant);
    NORWOOD, James 23 (son in law) (work
    in sawmill), Ada 19 (dau), Arthur
    3/12 (g son)
79. SOLOMAN, Andrew 33 (KY KY T), Sarah 30 (GA
    NC GA); YEARGIN, Archey 6 (son) (AL),
    Ada 10/12 (b. Jul) (dau) (T)
80. DANIEL, Robert 57 (SC SC SC), Jane 46 (T SC
    SC), Elmira 31 (dau), Wiley 21, Alvira
    18, Susan 17, John 15, Martha 12, Mary
    9, Robert 7, Porter 6, Laura 2
81. RICHARDSON, George 22 (T VA T), Mary 24,
    Fanny 1
82. CLARK, William 30 (T T NC), Martha 32,
    James 10, Idar 8 (dau), Charles 6,
    Bertia 4 (dau), Ferdinan 2

Hh#   Page 11, Dist. 6

83. HOUTS, Henry 40 (farmer & pentioner)
    (wounded in army--crippled) (T VA VA),
    Elizabeth 30, Harrett 13, Milton 11,
    Mary 8, James 6, Josiah 3, Matilda 1
84. JONES, Catherine 42 (widow) (VA VA VA),
    Martha 12 (T T VA), Ulysses 4 (T T VA)
85. SPRING, Benj. F. 62, Fainna 57, Carry 38
    (dau), William 28, Nicholas 22, Norah
    21, Lulah 16, James 14
86. DURHAM, Sarah 39 (widow), Drurah 19, John
    10, James 6
87. ANDERSON, Audly 75, Mary 65 (wife), James
    27, Roland 24
88. HART, Charles 36 (NY CT CT); AUSTIN, Eley
    28 (servant); BLACKBURN, Cesel (m) 23;
    AUSTIN, James 73 (laborer)
89. McREYNOLDS, Wed. S. 26, Mahaly 27 (wife),
    Willett 1 (dau)
90. SKILLEM, James (B) 30, Lean 25 (wife),
    Geneva 4, Walter 2, Elizabeth 3/12 (b.
    Mar)
91. BRIDGMAN, William (Mu) 30 (T NC NC), Sarah
    31 (GA GA GA), Albert 12 (T T T), Ar-
    minta 11, Florence 9, Martha 7, America
    3, McFerson 2/12 (b. Apr), Carroll 6
    (nephew), William 7 (nephew), Delphia
    (B) 57 (mother) (NC NC NC)

                    Page 12, Dist. 6

92. CHILDERS, Alexanders 28 (GA NC NC), Mary 26,
    William 8, Frances 6, Girty 4 (dau),
    Henry 3, Bascomb 3, Flora 2/12
93. HOGUE, James L. 50, Elizabeth 48, Sarah 22,
    Samuel 17, William 13, French 10;
    WALKER, Oliver 19 (nephew), John 18
    (nephew); HOGUE, Flavious 21 (house
    carpenter) (relationship omitted)
94. TWOFFORO?, James D. 50 (FL T T), Sarah 40
    (VA T T), Anthony 16, Amanda 13, Mary 9,
    James 7, Gerthy 5, Cavey 3 (dau),
    Gracey 1
95. HENSON, Elbert (B) 26, Mariah (Mu) 23 (T T
    AL), Emma 7, Hannah 6, Isaac 2, Mary
    6/12 (b. Dec)
96. ANGLE, Elizabeth 40, Bird 19 (son) (idiotic),
    Alice 16 (dau), Luke 10 (son) (idiotic),
    John 5 (son)
97. ROBERSON, Jane (B) 40 (widow), Coon 12 (son),
    Critt 16 (son)
98. McREYNOLDS, Alexander (Mu) 38, Caroline 32,
    William 15, Charles 12, Halley 3,
    Thursy 10/12 (b. Aug)
99. BROWDER, Alexander (B) 23, Amanda 18, Ema
    4

                    Page 13, Dist. 6

100. TULLOSS, Jack (B) 60 (GA GA GA), Beda 58
     (GA GA GA)
101. BROCK, James 21, Sarah 21, Mary 3, Laura 1
102. BROCK, William 27, Sarah 23; MERRITT, Scott
     19
103. CURTIS, Hezekiah 69, Lucinda 69, John 28,
     Mariah 35 (wife of son), Matilda 10 (g
     dau), Charles 8 (g son), Hezekiah 5 (g
     son), Matilda 3 (g dau), Cora 4/12 (b.
     Feb) (g dau)
104. BRIDGMAN, Anthony (Mu) 60 (widower) (VA VA
     T), James 21 (T VA T), George 18,
     William 16, Anthony 11, Adaline 13
105. BRIDGMAN, Tilda (Mu) 27 (dau--of Anthony?)
     (VA VA VA), Mary 6 (g dau) (T T VA),
     Sam 4 (g dau) (T T VA), Sam 4 (g son) (T
     T VA), James 1 (g son) (T T VA), Martha
     (B) 45 (boarding) (GA GA GA)
106. BRIDGMAN, Jack (B) 50 (neuralge) (AL AL AL),
     Clarissa 50, John 9, Clarissa 8;
     PITTS, Charles 45 (laborer) (rheumatism)
107. SWAFFORD, James 73 (gravel) (SC SC SC),
     Mary 60, John 39, Manervy 35 (wife of
     son), Thomas 17 (g son), Reuben 12 (g
     son), John 11 (g son), Emit 8 (g son),
     Joseph 7 (g son), Nancy 5 (g dau),
     Louisa 3 (g dau), Jane 1 (g dau)

Hh#	Page 13 (cont'd)

108. STEPP, John 39, Melvina 33, James 11, John 9 (deaf & dumb), Palestine 7, Henry 4, Moses 10/12 (b. Jul)

Page 14, Dist. 6

109. FRALEY, Johnathan 54 (T KY T), sarah 42, William 17, Mary 14, Alma 3; VERNON, Elizabeth 70 (mother in law) (widow), Martha 65 (boarder) (on crutches from fule)
110. RIGSBY, John 44, Ann 41 (T NC NC), Daniel 19, Robert 14, Franklin 12, Marion 8, Elizabeth 5
111. RIGSBY, Plesant 23, Martha 25, Charlotte 1
112. GREER, John (B) 20, Marth 18
113. McCLOUD, William 59, Kelzada 54, James 22, Isaac 19
114. LAWSON, Houston 29, Ann 20, Magaline 5, Gerta 4
115. IVEY, John (Mu) 31, Nancy 49 (mother), Catherine 20 (sis), Sophia 15 (sis), James 12 (bro?), Salinda 7 (sis)
116. SPRING, Rufus (Mu) 38, Letticia (B) 39, William (Mu) 15, Charles 13, James 9, Lawrence 7, Gallent 2, Rufus 1/12 (b. May)
117. BENNETT, Hosy (B) 50 (rheumatism--crippled), Harriett 49, Lewis 24 (deaf & dumb), Maranda 20, Matilda 18, Lucinda 14, Alexander 12, John 10, Bertha 3, James 5

Page 15, Dist. 6

118. SIMPSON, Peter 39 (GA NC GA), Elizabeth 29 (AL T T), William 14 (FL), Dolla 11 (dau) (T), Sarah 9, Louisa 8, Peral 5, James 1
119. PHILIP, Richard 23, Elizabeth 18
120. SPRING, Alexander (B) 24, Alice 23, Charles 5, Samuel 1
121. SHUMATE, John 30, Rhoda 24, Anna 4, John 2, Laura 9/12 (b. Sep)
122. SHUMATE, Thomas 48, Rachiel 49, Rufus 26, Lucius 24 (teacher), Hannah 85 (mother) (NC T T); SKILLERN, Laura 20 (servant)
123. BRIDGMAN, Edward (B) 46 (GA GA GA), Penelopa 45
124. MOORE, William 65 (widower), Letta 36, Lou 10 (dau), John 8, Gerta 5, William 5/12 (b. Jan)
125. BIRCH, Mahaly (Mu) 60 (widow) (T T NC), Sarah 39, James (B) 37
126. BOLTON, Lana (Mu) 60 (widow), Henry 22, Josa 15
127. SCHOOLFIELD, Matthew (B) 24, Matilda 21
128. SPRING, George (B) 40, Emila 25 (wife), William 8, Ida 3, Isaac 1

Page 16, Dist. 6

129. NAIL, Nelson (Mu) 61 (crippled) (T __ __), Mary 30 (wife) (T __ __)
130. COOPER, John 45 (PA PA PA), Margarett 38 (PA PA PA), Alferd 16 (PA PA PA), George P. 11 (T), Cora 4
131. LOYD, Roland P. 53 (T VA T), Margart 53, William 22, Mary 20, Margartt 18, Joseph 15, Sarah 12; SWAFFORD, Mark (B) 19
132. ROBERSON, James M. 64, Selila E. 35 (wife), Samul 12, Rufus 11, William 10, James 8, Margarett 6, Dorinda 3, Gordon 10/12 (b. Jun); HASKEW, Hezekiah 21 (laborer), Brown 19 (laborer)
133. McREYNOLD, Henry (B) 50, Hannah 40, James (Mu) (idiotic) 16, Selilah 14
134. WETHERBEE, Henry 64 (crippled) (NY Eng NY), Margaret 54 (PA PA PA), Cora 18 (MI), William 22 (MI), Rutha 17 (dau in law) (T), infant 1/12 (b. May) (g dau)

Hh#	Page 16 (cont'd)

135. RENFRO, George 54 (minister), Elizabeth 51, William 26, Nancy 24, Sarah 16, James 14
136. HALL, Thomas 46, Nancy 42, John 20, Hortense 15, Louvina 13, Harrison 10, Sarah 7, Clarence 5, Abby 1 (dau); OWENS, William 20

Page 17, Dist. 6

137. GREER, Moses 50 (VA VA IN), Orpha 47 (T VA T), Richard 22, Flora 19, Caroline 16, Madison? 13, Isa 11, Henry 6; ROBERSON, Matilda 41 (servant); GREER, Thomas 50 (bro)
138. GREER, William H. 59 (VA VA IN), Mahala 44, John 26, Martha 23, Nancy 18, Emma 16, Clay 14, Louella 11, Adda 7, Moses 3
139. McREYNOLDS, Alexander 54 (T VA T), Emila 52 (VA VA Ire), Gather 16 (T VA T), Martha 14 (T T VA), Ider 10 (dau)
140. FURGERSON, Mary 30 (dau--of #139?) (T T VA), Eugene 2 (g dau) (T T VA), Gertrude 5/12 (b. Jan) (g dau) (T T VA)
141. RIGSBY, James 46 (miller) (T NC T), Eliza 43, John 24, Washington 23, Raymond 20, James 17, Virginia 9, Julia 6
142. GAMBLE, William 52 (T T VA), Mary 44 (T VA T), William 11, Samuel 8, Charles 5, Martha 2; BLEVINS, William 20 (laborer), SULLIVAN, Richard 17 (laborer)
143. HENRY?, James 37 (PA PA PA), Emily A. 27, Mona 3, George 3/12 (b. Mar)

Page 18, Dist. 6

144. VERNON, James A. 54 (SC NC NC), Ann 54 (VA VA Ire), Gather 15 (son), Mary 13, Edna 11; ORME, Wetherson 26 (stepson) (school teacher) (T NC VA), Catherin 80 (step mother in law) (old age) (KY KY KY); GREER, Mary 78 (mother in law) (old age) (Ire Ire Ire); SWAFFORD, Anthony (B) 16 (laborer)
145. DANIEL, Syrus 26, Eliza 20, James 2
146. STEP, Perry 50, Elton 47 (wife), Rutha 26, Adaline 16, Bell 15, John 12, Margaret 9, Ezell 7
147. TULLOP, Henry (B) 29, Jane 27, Flora 10, James 9, Frank 6, Alexander 5, Emmerson 4, Calla 2 (dau), Preston 1
148. SKILLEM, James A. 41 (T VA T), Caroline 36 (T GA GA), James Ross 12, John C. 10, Neal S. 8, Lether F. 6 (dau), Mather 11/12 (b. Jul) (dau)
149. BRIDGMAN, Richard (Mu) 35, Jane 32; HIXON, Fountain 15 (laborer)
150. LEA, Emila 54 (f), Loftus L. 22 (son) (AL), Martha P. 22 (AL), Lankford 18 (AL)
151. STEPHENS, Bird (Mu) 40 (T T GA), Mariah (B) 35, Nancy 15, James 13, Adaline (Mu) 11, William 7, Lawrence 4 (B)

Page 19, Dist. 6

152. ROBERSON, Jeremiah (B) 43, Mary 35, Ida 16, John 11, Samuel 8, Peter 7, William 4, Sarah 2, Florence 4/12 (b. Feb)
153. HUDSON, Robert H. 65 (T NC SC), Emila F. 57 (T VA VA), Sarah 25, Martha 23, David 21, Margaret 19, Fannah 16, Elizabeth 13, Richard 11
154. SKILLEM, William 57 (T VA VA), Sarah 47 (T VA VA), Charles 9
155. SKILLEM, Jesse (B) 55 (VA VA VA), Susan 55 (VA VA VA), Rachiel 22, Jessee 18, Elizabeth 16, William 12

Dist. 7

156. LAWSON, Lyra 56, Charlotta 54 (wife), Franklin 20, Manervia 19, Charles 12, Elizabeth 8
157. BURCH, Franklin (Mu) 41 (KY T T), May Jane 45

Hh#   Page 19 (cont'd)

158. SULLIVAN, Franklin 41, Catherine 38, Henry
     18, Mary 15, Sarah 13, William 11,
     Martha 8, Corabelle 4, James 2, John
     6/12 (b. Dec)
159. GREER, Henry (B) 29, Zilpha 28, Ellen 2,
     Margarett 2/12 (b. May)

                Page 20, Dist. 7

160. SWAFFORD, Green (B) 54, Angeline 25 (wife),
     Sarah 7, Ralph 5, Samul 4, William 12,
     Wilson 10, Mary 5 (g dau)
161. WORTHINGTON, Lewis (B) 23, Elizabeth 25,
     Elizabeth 4, James 1
162. McDANIEL, Thomas (B) 23, Pauline 22, Ida 2,
     Flora 9/12 (b. Oct)
163. SPRING, Martha (B) 38 (widow), Florene 12,
     Charles 11, Martha 9, Webster 7
164. SPEARS, Taylor (Mu) 28, Sarah (B) 25, Jane
     5, Thursy (Mu) 3 (dau), Lawrence 1;
     BRIDGMAN, Guseman (B) 13 (laborer)
165. RANEY, Nancy 55 (widow), Laurah 21, infant
     1 (f)
166. FARMER, Squilla 51, Mary 50, William 26,
     John 24, Martin 22, James 17, Martha
     15, Permelia 13, Erastus 7; CASTELLER,
     Micheil 20 (boarder); HEDGLEY, William
     36 (boarder) (stone cutter) (Eng Wales
     Eng)
167. BRIDGMAN, Mariah (B) 52 (widow); SKILLEM,
     Sarah 8 (cozin)
168. RUTLEDGE, Benjamin 26, Delila 24, Lanora 4,
     Reason 2
169. WILSON, Charles 31, Elvira 31, William 13,
     Matilda 11, John Raymond 3, Luther 8/12
     (b. Oct); FOSTER, William 21 (nephew)

                Page 21, Dist. 7

170. FURGERSON, James 41 (blacksmith), Elizabeth
     43, Charles 16, Polk 14, Frank 12,
     Nicholas 10, Juley 8, Allice 7, Sidney
     5, Samul 2
171. McREYNOLDS, Saml. M. 50 (rheumatism) (T VA
     T), Kate 35 (wife), Charles 21, Hally
     10 (dau); BELL, Clarissa 37 (sis in
     law) (teacher); REEDY, Nancy 29
     (servant), Henry 3 (servant's son)
172. HENNIGAR, Marcus O. 33, Eliza E. 29, Charles
     8, Lilla May 5, Francis 3, Emet 1
173. HALL, Cintha 60 (widow), Lewis 29, Mar-
     garett 37, Susan 31, Jacob 20, James
     11 (g son), William 6 (g son), Johny
     11 (g son)
174. DURHAM, Lucinda 36 (widow) (T VA NC),
     Drury 17, John 10, James 5
175. BURNETT, Nicholas 57 (miller) (T VA T),
     Manervia H. 45, Emma 22, Sarah 19,
     William 17 (one eye out), Jeremiah 14,
     Mary 12, Elanor 10, Martha 8, John 6,
     Estella 1

                Page 22, Dist. 7

176. KEEDY, Virginia 69 (widow) (cancer on face)
     (T VA VA)
177. KEENER, Wayman 24, Martha 23, Martha 4,
     James 1; SMITH, Matilda 13 (wife's
     sis)
178. ROBERSON, William 31, Mary 33 (T T VA),
     Catherine 10, Orpha 8, Martha J. 6,
     Richard 4, Tulloss 2 (son), Butler
     6/12 (b. Nov)
179. ROBERSON, John R. 33, Mary 21, Moses 3,
     James 1, Catharine 72 (mother)
180. CAMPBELL, Obediah 29 (SC SC SC), Mary 26
     (T VA T), Allice 5, Frances 4, Virginia
     2, Foster 6/12 (b. Oct) (son)
181. ROBERSON, Adam 35, Louisa 28, Marilda 10,
     Martha 8, Salla 4, Wiley 1
182. INGRAM, Mary 57 (widow), Charles 13
183. RUTLEDGE, Jane 58 (widow) (T NC MD), Ander-
     son 21, Edwin 19, Wily 18
184. EVERETT, David 32, Mary 28 (T T OH), Thomas
     3; MATTHEWS, Mary 58 (mother in law)
     (OH PA SC)

Hh#   Page 22 (cont'd)

185. KEEDY, Nancy 56 (widow) (T VA T), Sarah 30,
     Nancy 29, Susan 25, John 18, Caroline
     14, Emaline 12, Thomas 13, Alfred 10,
     Taylor 7 (g son); MASSY, Robert 2 (g
     son)

                Page 23, Dist. 7

186. SUTHERLAND, Alexander 33, Sarah 38, Adda 5
187. RUTLEDGE, Lorenzo 27 (T VA T), Nancy 25,
     Emit A. 2, Hester Ann 1
188. SUTHERLAND, James 29, Mary 25, Nancy 10,
     James 8, Emaline 6, William 4, Sarah 2
189. SUTHERLAND, Thomas 56 (T VA VA), Emaline 56
     (NC NC NC), David 14, Nancy 12
190. SPRING, James (Mu) 42, Catharine 36, Samul
     16, Lucy Ann 14, John 10
191. HAWKINS, Pinkney 23 (NC NC NC), Mary 20,
     Hatti (T T T), Mary 1 (T T T)
192. BLEVINS, Joseph 27 (T VA KY), Mary Jane 25,
     Sarah C. 1
193. WOOTON, Samuel 50, Lucinda 50, Samuel 17,
     Isaac 14, Plesant 14, Charles 12,
     Coldony 11, Lafayette 8
194. THOMPSON, Alfred 23, America 22, Mary Ann 2
195. GANT, Daniel (B) 38, Emaline 18 (Mu) (wife),
     George (B) 1
196. SWAFFORD, Hezekiah 22
197. BOLTON, James 24, Margarett 21, Emma 4,
     Jessey 2, Anetta 6/12

                Page 24, Dist. 7

198. ROBERSON, William (B) 35, Sarah 30 (VA T T),
     Alexander 14 (son), John 12, Ada 10,
     Ider 8 (dau), Charles 7, Savanah 6,
     James 4, Samul 3, William 11/12 (b. May)
199. PANKY, Benjamin (B) 30 (T T VA), Catharine
     35 (NC NC NC); HOWARD, Mary 15 (servant),
     PANKEY, Henry 13 (laborer); SCHOOLFIELD,
     Thomas 8 (nephew)
200. BELL, David R. 42 (AL T NC), Mary E. 26
     (wife), Ida 7, William 3, Kate 3/12 (b.
     Feb), Nancy 68 (mother) (old age) (NC
     NC VA); PANKY, Alexander (B) 10
     (servant)
201. BOMAN, David 52, Emaline 46, Mary 14, Lemuel
     18
202. BILLINGSLEY, Fanny (B) 30 (GA GA GA), Cally
     (Mu) 6 (dau) (T T GA), Charles 4,
     Eugene (B) 1; ALLEN, John 82 (boarder)
     (old age) (Scot Scot Scot)
203. LEA, Louansa 64 (T KY SC), Terry 49 (bro)
     (T KY SC), Rufus 47 (bro) (rheumatism)
     (T KY SC); FURGERSON, Anna 14 (servant);
     HASKEW, William 19 (laborer); BLEVINS,
     Esquire? 17 (laborer)
204. LEA, Eliza Ann 52 (widow) (NC NC VA);
     STINSON, Sarah 11 (servant) (T VA VA);
     COOK, Lucien 71 (boarder) (VT NH CT)
205. THURMAN, Isaac 31, Louiza 24, Maybell 4,
     Ross 1
206. CHILDERS, Andrew 40 (T NC NC), Sarah 36,
     Laura 12, Joseph 11, Virginia 9, Ar-
     minta 7, Luther 4, Ira 2

                Page 25, Dist. 7

207. LOVELADY, James 45, Rebecca 40, Sarah 18,
     Madison 16, John 14, Daniel 12, Thomas
     10, Fanny 2
208. WHITTENBURG, Scott 35, Amanda 32, Elizabeth
     9, Alexander 8, James 3, Hatta 1
209. SULLIVAN, William 65, Elizabeth 54
210. McGAN, Susan 56 (widow) (T T SC), John R. 24,
     Anna 16 (T Ire T)
211. READ, Kezziah 45 (widow), Franklin 20,
     Samul 18
212. McGAN, Polk 26, May Ann 22
213. HALE, Richard 65, Adaline 52, William 16
     (deformed), John 13, Thursey 6 (dau)
214. SULLIVAN, Matilda 30, Alexander 12,
     Virginia 6, Nancy 4
215. MOORE, Jesse 25, Marilda 24, William 6, Olla
     3, Calvin 1

Hh#	Page 25 (cont'd)

216. FERGERSON, Margarett 55 (widow), Terry 22, Adda 18, George 16
217. BENNET, Roscow (B) 24, Louanza 25, Henry 10 (son), Alexander 8, James 8, Tobe 5 (son), Martha 7/12

Page 26, Dist. 7

218. TETERS, John 39, Sarah 31, Emma 9, Nancy 7, Martha 6, James 4, Penelopa 3
219. HENRY, John W. 47 (widower) (PA PA PA), Alonzo 20 (PA PA PA), Edgar 14 (KS?), Lilly May 12 (DE), Dora 8 (DE), Charles 10 (DE), Bertram 2 (dau) (T), Flora 8/12 (b. Sep)
220. ZIGLER, William 36 (T VA T), Catharine 30, William 5
221. GREGOREY, James 32, Anna 32 (CT CT CT), Emma 7, Laura 4, Sarah 1; MILTS, James 23 (laborer)
222. McJUNKINS, Andrew 28, Nancy 19 (wife), William 2, John 4/12 (b. Jan)
223. GREEN, George 53, Margarett 45, Albion 22 (son) (white swelling), John 11, Mary 6
224. KING, Atrum T. 37 (NC NC NC), Margarett 30, Annett 5 (dau), Ethel 3
225. McREYNOLDS, Isaac 34, Adda 32, Tulloss 11 (son), Samul 8, Thomas 31 (bro), Janet? 28 (bro's wife), Walter 6 (bro's son), John B. 4 (bro's son), Magga 2 (bro's dau); SHUMATE, Margarett 33 (servant); LOZA, John (B) 20 (laborer); HIXON, Allen (B) 18

Page 27, Dist. 7

226. HALL, Ferrell 40, Martha 35, John 18, Sarah 14, Ann 11, Netta 8, Dalta 4 (dau), Elbert 2
227. HARWOOD, Benj. 38, Alzera 28, Margarett 8, Simeon 3, James 9/12 (b. Oct)
228. LEWIS, Simon D. 45, Nancy 45, Josa 18, Ersa 15, Matta 13, Peter 10, Jacob 6, Dario 2
229. McCULY, Thomas 45, Margarett 45, Emma 19, Nanny 14, Mary 9, Elmona 6 (son), Minna 3, Magga 1 (dau)
230. PHILIPS, Elizabeth 48 (widow), Jacob 21, John 18; OWENS, Mary 76 (mother)
231. FURGERSON, Mitt 60, Sarah 50 (wife), Samul 20, William 18, Abner 16, Daniel 11, John 9
232. KEEDY, William 29, Tennessee 23, Alice 5, Selina 3, Lewis 1; HUMBLE, Isaac 73 (relationship omitted)

Page 28, Dist. 7

233. RUSSELL, Edmond 80 (pentioner) (blind) (NC NC NC), Emaline 45 (wife) (T T KY)
234. JORDON, Asa 104 (old age) (GA NC NC), Grisella 87 (wife) (SC PA PA)
235. SWAFFORD, James 20, Louisa 18, John 1
236. CONLEY, John W. 31 (T T SC), Lucy 33 (NC NC NC), William 12, Tatte 7 (son), Nancy 6
237. RITCHEY, David 30 (T T AL), Sarah 6 (dau), Vestino 4 (dau), Serepta 32 (wife) (T T NC)
238. GREGORY, Thomas 43, Sarah 23 (wife), Louisa 13, Mary 11, John 8, James P. 4, Birtha 11/12 (b. Aug); SPEARS, James 24 (laborer)
239. McDANIEL, Tolbert 37 (wood work of wagon maker), Margaret 32 (AL AL AL), James 13, Samul 10, Mary 8, Charles 6, Lizza 4 (rheumatism), Robert 2, John 7/12 (b. Nov)
240. VANN, James M. 51, Jane 53 (NC NC NC), George 16, Emaline 13, James 12, Bird 7 (g son)
241. RITCHEY, Joseph 26, Sarah 18, Thursy 1 (dau)
242. GRIMSLEY, Abraham 59, Emaline 58, Elizabeth 26 (teacher), William 10

Hh#	Page 28 (cont'd)

243. GRIMSLY, James M. 38, Sarah 31, Walter 6, Lester 2

Page 29, Dist. 7

244. SPEARS, John 30 (teacher), Caroline 29, Alta 2
245. CAMPBELL, Eli 23, Martha 23, John 2, Elizabeth 5/12
246. PRITCHETT, James 67 (NC NC NC), Sciota 65 (T T NC); HAVEY, Margaret 16 (servant)
247. MORGAN, Thomas 32, Susan 34, George 12, Jessee 10, Mary 8, Isaac 6, Kittie 4, Minnie 3/12 (b. Mar)
248. WINSETT, William 38, Illa 39 (wife), Corda 12, William 10, Emitt 6, Olla 4 (dau), Ethel 2

Page 1, Dist. 8

1. ROGERS, William 28, Matilda S. 27, James 5, Mary 3
2. ROGERS, John 32; SMITH, Sarah 55 (mother) (asthma), Elizabeth 15 (sis) (T VA T); JORDAN, Martha J. 43 (servant)
3. SMITH, Rachel 47 (widow), Amanda J. 22 (T VA T), Julia A. 20 (T VA T), Samuel 3 (g son)
4. REAL, Charles 47 (VA VA VA), Margaret L. (T VA T), James 18, Mary A. 14, Elizabeth A. 13, John 11, George B. 8, Sarah L. 5, Caroline T. 3, Solomon J. 11/12 (b. Jun); TURNER, Mary 67 (mother in law)
5. FORLEY, J. J. 53 (T VA KY), Sarah 53 (wife) (T VA T), Robert L. 11
6. FORLEY, John 30, Mary 26, Sarah 5, Jabee 4 (son), John 1
7. FORLEY, Thomas H. 24, Orletha 20
8. FORLEY, Patton 22, Eedy A. 24
9. ALEXANDER, Stephen H. 58 (carpenter & mill wright) (T NC NC), Mary J. 39 (wife) (T GA T), Lovenia F. 28 (dau) (AL), James A. 13 (T), Stephen H. 12, Sarah J. 9, Thomas H. 7, Ceney L. 2 (dau), Elen 10/12

Page 2, Dist. 8

1. ROBERSON, Peter (B) 41, Martha 25 (wife), Samuel 19 (son), Rufus 15, Elizabeth 14, Peter 6, Polly 4, John Lafayett 3, Ernest E. 1; TULLOSS, Alfred 16 (relationship omitted)
2. PERIN, S. E. 29 (GA T T), Emeline 27, Miller F. 5, Isaac B. 9/12 (b. Aug)
3. THURMAN, W. A. 35, Octava 35 (NC NC NC), Ida F. 4, Hester A. 2
4. PRICE, John 41 (NC NC NC), Thomas 26 (bro) (T NC NC), Mary 30 (sis) (NC NC NC), HUMBLE, Lovina 46 (sis) (widow) (NC NC NC), Wyatt 21 (nephew) (T NC NC), Virginia 18 (niece) (T NC NC)
5. PRICE, Delila 37 (widow), Nancy 19, John T. 18, James 17, William 4 (g son)
6. PEMBERTON, Alfred 31 (GA VA VA), Nancy J. 39, Mary E. 11, Isaac N. 8, Thomas 5, Elizabeth 3
7. BLEVINS, Samuel 48, Malinda 46 (T NC T), Hugh 18, Gustavus 14, William 12, Francis 10, Susan 7, Thomas 2
8. BATES, Henry (B) 46 (NC NC SC), Mary 35 (NC NC NC), Annis C. 16 (dau) (GA), Mary L. 12 (T), John 10, Adeline 7, George 4

Page 3, Dist. 8

1. HENSON, Lafayette (B) 19 (married within yr), Martha 19 (GA NC NC), William 1/12 (b. Apr)
2. MERRIMAN, Dianner 69 (widow) (SC SC VA), George 25 (T T SC)
3. BROCK, D. H. 62 (tending grist mill) (SC SC SC), Jiney 62 (wife) (T T VA); MANREY, John 5 (g son); WARD? Elizabeth 22 (dau) (divorced), Mary C. 7 (g dau) (T NC T), Sarah 6 (g dau) (T NC T)

Hh#   Page 3 (cont'd)

4. BROCK, John 21 (T SC T), Leomy 20 (wife), Elbert 4, Gather 1

5. THURMAN, Matilda J. 52 (widow) (T VA T), Wyatt 23, Laura 20, Wile 14 (son), Lorenzo 12 (dau), Ida 8

6. HICKENBOTTON, John 23, Martha 26, James 2, William H. 1/12 (b. Apr); RANEY, Nancy 55 (mother in law)

7. HASKEW, William 68 (T VA NC), Telitha 70 (NC SC NC); WELBORN, Joseph A. 16 (g son) (T MS T); STINSON, Mary 40 (relationship omitted) (widow) (VA VA VA); SMITH, Henry 18 (relationship omitted)

8. HASKEW, Mary 40 (widow) (T NC T), Hezekiah 20, Samuel B. 18, Joseph B. 16

9. ROGERS, William C. 48 (farmer & merchant) (T VA SC), Anna J. 38, Byron 19, William F. 17, John A. 16, Lula 12, Lola 12, Isaac A. 10, Hester A. 6

10. ONEAL, Samuel 26 (shoe maker) (T VA VA), Jane 25, Laura B. 9, John 7, Alexander 5, Josephine 3

Page 4, Dist. 8

1. FORD, Elizabeth A. 47 (divorced), Margaret F. 21, Lillie A. 20; CRAVENS, Sarah F. 65 (aunt)

2. HENNINGER, F. A. 59 (T VA VA), Elba 57 (T NC VA), Julia 20, Benjamin 18, Gertrude 15

3. ANDERSON, W. A. 41 (farmer & merchant), Catherine E. 39 (NJ NH NJ), Emma I. 12, Ella J. 10, Walter E. 8, Effa May 6, Archie T. 4, Arthur G. 1

4. STEPHENS, W. E. 31 (professor in college) (T T VA), Elizabeth 24, Mary 2; CARROLL, Lewis 17 (boarder) (TX TX TN)

5. HOLLAND, Thomas 29 (AL T AL), Margaret 29, Cora Jane 10, Jack 4, Albert 2, Henry L. 3/12 (b. Mar); DILL, Newton 15 (relationship omitted)

6. LAMB, John K. 28, Margaret C. 17 (wife), Adam C. 1

7. STOUT, William D. 42 (physician), Nancy E. 36, Ransom L. 11, Robert C. 10, Rufus K. 8, James 5, Simma R. 3 (dau)

8. STOUT, Elbert K. 28

9. SCHOOLFIELD, Perry A. 40 (blacksmith), Mary C. 41, Martha E. 18, Emma C. 13, Nancy M. 10, David R. 8, Curry R. 6, Ethel T. 7/12 (b. Oct), Etel H. (f) 7/12 (b. Oct); HASKEW, Samuel T. 16 (nephew)

Page 5, Dist. 8

1. SKILLERN, Alfred 63 (hauling produce to market), Mary 31 (dau), David 13 (son), Catherine 11, Effa 2

2. HOLLAND, Leroy 25, Matilda 21 (sis)

3. BUTLER, John W. 51 (T NC NC), Nancy M. 38 (wife), William V. 13, Sally E. 11, John L. 8

4. THOMPSON, Leroy 45, Mary 36 (wife) (T KY KY), Martha J. 12, James L. 10 (sick headache), George W. 5, Archie 3, Samuel H. 5/12 (b. Dec)

5. SMITH, Isaac 45, Mary J. 30, James 7, Martha 2

6. MERRIMAN, Allen R. 46 (NC NC NC), Margaret 40 (T KY NC), Almira T. 23 (dau--this name crossed out on schedule), Alice E. 21, Eliza A. 19, Florida J. 16, Florence M. 15, James Wm. 13, Isaac R. 10, Margaret O. 7, Rufus V. 4

7. ROBERSON, Polk 35 (T KY NC), Phila A. 23 (wife), Isaack K. 2, Roy D. 1, John R. 45 (bro) (stock herder) (T KY NC), Elvira 75 (mother) (NC NC NC), Douglas 7 (son)

8. SMITH, Martha 30, Margaret 15 (dau), Isaac 13, Thomas 10 (eats dirt), William 7, James 5, Lewis 1

Hh#   Page 6, Dist. 8

1. STANDIFER, W. L. 36, Mary 33 (T NC T), John M. 12, Naoma 9, Penelope 6, Josie 5, Edith 2, Edna 2, Esther 11/12 (b. Jun)

2. BOYD, Benjaman F. 33 (farmer & carpenter), Margaret A. 27, Willis B. 4, Wily B. 2, _____ 5/12 (b. Dec) (son)

3. HOWARD, James J. 29, Evaline C. 27

4. BOYD, Right J. 26, Caroline 54 (mother)

5. BOYD, William J. 59 (T GA T), Margaret 59 (T NC NC), Mary J. 26 (T T NC), Samuel L. 21 (T T NC), Drucilla 20 (T T NC), George D. 15 (T T NC), Drucilla 34 (sis) (T T T)

6. BOYD, George W. 40 (T GA T), Martha 35, Mary C. 13, James M. 11, Frances 5, Napoleon 2, Dee 8/12 (b. Sep) (son)

7. SAVAGE, Lucinda 60 (widow) (T NC VA); TURNER, Samuel 19 (son), Margaret 20 (dau)

8. RAINEY, Mary A. 54 (T NC VA), John 87 (father) (NC NC NC)

9. SMITH, William Mc. 45, Mary 27 (wife), Thomas 7, Phily 4 (dau), Mary 2, Nilla? 3/12 (b. Feb), Martha 20, Delila 17, Susanna 14

Page 7, Dist. 8

1. RAINS, Mahala 49 (widow), Right 17, Joseph 14, James 12, Crocia 10 (dau), William 8

2. TURNER, John D. 29, Nettie 24, Edward F. 3, Samuel L. 2, Ernest 7/12 (b. Oct)

3. RAINS, Marlen 57 (T VA NC), Milla E. 53 (T GA NC), Drucill E. 20, Manela M. 18 (dau), William 14, Leonidas 12

4. STOUT, Mary J. 32 (widow) (T T VA), Martha L. 12, Edgar F. 11 (consumption), Emma I. 10, Ella A. 10, Thomas L. 6, Thursay A. 4 (dau)

5. DYE, James 33 (NC NC NC), Anna 23 (T VA T), Alfred B. 10 (son)

6. POPE, J. T. 33, Cordelia F. 24 (wife) (T VA T), Lulah 2, Emma 5/12 (b. Dec)

7. DYE, Obediah 45 (NC NC NC), Syntha 38 (T NC SC), Ailey 79 (mother) (NC NC NC)

8. DYE, Perry 38 (NC NC NC), Mary J. 38, Calvin 18, Obediah 10, Adar 2 (dau)

9. SUTHERLAND, G. W. 48, Ellen 47 (T VA T), William S. 22, John L. 19, Samuel 16, James P. 11 (idiotic), Trous G. 7 (son), Flora Ellen 3; SEALS, Stacy A. 20 (dau), Charles A. 1 (g son)

Page 8, Dist. 8

1. STOUT, John 61 (T VA T), Louisa J. 44 (wife), Berry B. 25 (son), Christopher S. 17, Louisa T. 14, Jesse N. 11, Amos B. 9, Ira N. 6, Margaret E. 2

2. TURNER, Kosouth 29, Margaret 29 (wife), Samuel 6, Neona 2

3. HALL, John 69 (T VA VA), Permelia J. 53 (wife) (T NC T); MURPHY, John B. 85 (father in law) (blacksmith) (NC MD NC)

4. ALEXANDER, Sarah B. 60 (widow) (VA VA VA), Leonidas E. 22 (T VA VA), Lucius H. 18

5. ANDERSON, James F. 33, Martha L. 25, Esther L. 2, Alta 1

6. ALEXANDER, William 29 (house carpenter) (AL T AL), Rachel 29, Adeline 4, Ellen 3

7. KEEDY, Jacob 58 (blacksmith) (T MD T), Delila 57 (T NC T), Tennessee 19, Jacob 18, Richard 16, Delila 11

8. SMITH, Mary (Mu) 40 (widow) (snagged leg), William L. 23, Sarah A. 16, John T. 12, Backner 5

9. SMITH, Patrick (Mu) 19 (married within yr), Melissa 23 (wife); GOURENS, Vaney A. 5 (step dau), William 3 (step son)

10. HEARD, James C. 40 (farmer & merchant) (T T NC), Sarah A. 35 (T T NC), Melinda 17, Oceola 14 (son), Dora 11, William J. 5, Rebecca F. 3

Hh#   Page 9, Dist. 8

1. WALKER, Jeremiah 63, Sarah A. 64 (T T VA);
    DAY, Mary 25 (house maid) (VA VA VA),
    Hattie 4 (relationship omitted) (T
    VA VA); SMITH, Timothy 13 (relation-
    ship omitted)
2. WALKER, William 35, Mary 32; BOYD, Julia 26
    (relationship omitted), Byron B. 4
    (deaf & dumb)
3. GREER, Alexander C. 31 (T SC T), Rachel I.
    28 (T T NC), Lillis 8 (dau), Sally 6,
    Matta M. 4, James S. 2
4. DYE, Perry 22 (T T NC), Tennessee 22, John
    5, Mary Jane 1
5. SHANNON, Thomas 28 (T T NC), Sarah E. 30,
    Thomas 3, Susanna 68 (mother) (NC NC
    NC), Linda J. 12 (niece), Penelope S.
    (b. May) (dau)
6. HATFIELD, Robert B. 20 (married within yr),
    Rebecca E. 19
7. WALKER, Benjamin F. 29 (house carpenter &
    farmer), Laura 28 (T T VA), Edgar 9,
    Effie 7, Ernest 2
8. WALKER, James 65 (miller) (T NC SC), Rebec-
    ca 56, Tilmon J. 25, Martha 23 (dau
    in law), Allie J. 3 (g dau), Amy L. 1
    (g dau)
9. CAMPBELLE, John 25, Jane 18 (wife), Eliza-
    beth 6/12 (b. Nov); CLIFTON, Sally 31
    (sis in law)
10. HOXSON, Henninger 30, Hester Ann 28, Walter
    B. 2, Lela 8/12 (b. Sep)

                Page 10, Dist. 8

1. ROYAL, John 16, Mary 17 (wife) (GA GA GA),
    John 8/12 (b. Sep)
2. WALKER, George W. 38 (dentist & farmer) (T
    T NC), Sarah M. 36 (T NC T), William
    E. 12; HATFIELD, Margaret J. 4
    (relationship omitted)
3. HATFIELD, Taylor 36, Nancy 49 (wife),
    Thomas 19, Susanna 16, James 12,
    Margaret I. 10, John 7, Jane 5, Fanny
    1
4. COOLEY, Philip 38, Mary 38 (T T AL), Thomas
    14, John 10, James 8, Bethana 4,
    Newton 1
5. HOWARD, George W. 37 (shoe maker); POPE,
    Mary E. 37 (relationship omitted)
    (AR T T), Virginia T. 16 (relationship
    omitted)
6. HOWARD, Reason D. 40, Harriet E. 31 (T VA
    T), Margaret J. 1, Thomas B. 4/12
    (b. Jan); BOYD, Josie F. 9 (relation-
    ship omitted)
7. COOLEY, Jesse 32, Martha 30, Delotha J. 7,
    John 5, Mary E. 3
8. HOWARD, Buckner 76 (shoemaker) (T NC NC),
    Sally 64 (T MD VA); KEEDY, Zachariah
    T. 31 (nephew); SMITH, Delila 15
    (relationship omitted)
9. JOHNSON, Thomas 27, Sarah 20, Mary E. 2,
    James 1, Syntha 55 (mother), Monroe
    15 (bro)

                Page 11, Dist. 8

1. HIXSON, Thomas J. 28, Rebecca M. 28, Mattie
    L. 7, Mary E. 2; JONES, Benjamin F.
    21 (bro in law)
2. SMITH, Isaac N. 51 (VA ___), Delila R. 44
    (T VA T), Thomas B. 23, Houston 21,
    Penelope A. 18, Lenora F. 10, Isaac N.
    8, William A. 5, Alice K. 7/12 (b.
    Oct); REED, Margaret J. 25 (dau)
    (widow), Sarah F. 5 (g dau)
3. BOWLIN, Edmund (Mu) 75 (T VA VA), Delila J.
    50 (hurt by fall on stump)
4. HUNT, Lucinda 45 (widow) (T SC T); CARR,
    William 88 (cousin) (T VA SC); SMITH,
    Mary 26 (dau) (widow) (T NC T),
    Joseph 5 (g son), Levander 4 (g son),
    Vesta 3 (g dau), Minerva 2 (g dau),
    Simon 4/12 (b. Feb) (g son)

Hh#   Page 11 (cont'd)

5. GOWENS, John (Mu) 63, Louisa 50, Delila 26,
    Matilda 23, Martha 15, Harriet 10 (g
    dau), Aaron 8 (g son), Audley 8 (g son),
    Napoleon 6 (g son), Alfred 3 (g son),
    Wylie 1 (g son), Asbury 4 (g son),
    Eveline 1 (g dau)
6. GOWENS, Alfred (Mu) 22, Arminda (W) 20
    (wife)
7. KIZZIAH, George 29, Milla 29 (wife) (KY VA T),
    Joseph T. 4, John F. 2
8. SMITH, Nancy 26, George 6 (son)
9. BOWLIN, Orlean (Mu) 41 (f), Margaret 13
    (dau)

                Page 12, Dist. 8

1. BOWLIN, Lynda (Mu) 38, Alice 22 (dau),
    Lawrence 20 (son), James 15, John 13
2. BRITT, George 19, Margaret 28 (wife), Nancy
    4/12 (b. Jan)
3. BOWMAN, William T. 22 (KY KY KY), Mary E.
    21 (T T VA), John H. 2
4. BOWMAN, Afred M. 20 (married within yr) (KY
    KY KY), Martha J. 19 (T T VA)
5. CARSON, Rheubin 33 (GA NC NC), Amanda M. 29
    (GA GA GA), Emma 10, Rembert 9, Franklin
    7, Hester 4, William 2, Virgil 1
6. SMITH, Peter 48 (VA VA VA), Mary 30 (sis)
    (VA VA VA)
7. SMITH, John 60 (VA VA VA)
8. BROWN, Joseph 36 (NY Ger Ger), Matilda 45
    (wife), Milla E. 18 (dau), James 15,
    John 12, Margaret 8, Azariah 5, Tandy
    2
9. SMITH, William 35 (VA VA VA), Melissa 36
    (T VA VA), Mary E. 9
10. JAMES, Tandy 39, Martha J. 32, Elizabeth A.
    12, Laura E. 4; PIERCE, John 56 (father
    in law)

                Page 13, Dist. 8

1. BARGER, William T. 35 (T GA T), Sarah E. 29
    (KY VA KY), Mary J. 8 (KY), Minnie 6
    (KY), James 4 (KY), Ida 1 (T)
2. BOWMAN, Isaac 27 (KY KY KY), Virginia 30 (T
    VA VA), Melissa E. 6, Mary S. 4, James
    H. 2, Hester 3/12 (b. Feb); SMITH, Sally
    13 (dau) (T VA T)
3. SKILES, Joseph 24 (married within yr),
    Martha 16 (wife)
4. JAMES, Hezekiah S. 60, Margaret 38 (wife) (T
    VA VA), Samuel 18, Grant 16, Sarah 14,
    Mary 8, Tandy 6, Peter 4
5. JAMES, Malvina 44 (widow), William W. 22,
    David A. 20, John C. 18, Tandy 16 (has
    fits), Daniel A. 14, Charlie 12, Alonzo
    N. 8, Walter B. 7, George W. 4
6. ROGERS, Riley R. 52 (T VA T), Sarah A. 56
    (KY VA KY), Martha J. 27 (TX);
    MARLER, Edgar 7 (adopted)
7. BOWMAN, Ellis H. 50 (NC NC T), Jane 48,
    Mary E. 20, Sarah T. 15, Margaret A.
    13, Emmet H. 10, Ellar A. 6 (dau)
8. BOWMAN, John R. 27 (T NC T), Eliza 23, Emma
    1
9. JORDAN, George W. 29 (divorced) (T VA KY),
    Levina 71 (mother) (KY T T)

                Page 14, Dist. 8

1. GAD, Ansel 66 (T NC NC), Margaret 67 (SC FL
    FL)
2. GAD, Jethro 53, Polly 49 (T T SC)
3. GAD, John D. 36 (T T SC), Matilda 35, John B.
    18 (son), Mary M. 16, Ansel M. 14,
    William J. 12, Floyd 9, Martha 7, Rutha
    4, Charles 2; DENNIS, Isham 48 (uncle)
    (T SC SC)
4. BEAN, John W. 45 (VA VA VA), Maryann 45 (T
    T SC), Sarah C. 18, William B. 16,
    Jacob N. 14, Addie Jane 12, John W. 10,
    Mary A. 7, Charles D. 4

Hh#	Page 14 (cont'd)

5. BARGER, Hugh 31 (T GA T), Martha J. 28 (KY KY KY), John W. 7 (KY), Robert B. 4 (KY), Eddy R. 2 (KY), Jasper N. 11/12 (b. Jul) (T), Robert B. 67 (father) (GA T GA), Ellen 67
6. BRANNUM, William 34, Caldona E. 20, Mary A. 8/12 (b. Aug); VANDERGRIFF, John 18 (bro in law)
7. MILLER, Roland P. 22 (T T VA), Virginia C. 21, William J. 9/12 (b. Aug)
8. HALL, William 50 (widower), Sarah J. 26, Annis 16 (dau), James A. 14
9. REAL, George W. 28 (VA VA NC), Ann 63 (mother) (NC NC NC)
10. REAL, Solomon 26 (T VA NC), Sarah A. 12 (niece) (T T VA)
11. SMITH, John 23, Caroline 22 (T VA NC), Alonzo 3/12 (b. Feb)

Page 15, Dist. 8

1. REAL, Peter 34 (VA VA NC), Mary 26, William E. 3, Matilda J. 11/12 (b. Jun); SHANNON, Sally 11 (relationship omitted)
2. SKILES, Jacob 76 (T VA VA), Susanna 74, Jacob 34, Polly 38, Susanna 35, Jane 41
3. SKILES, Jeferson 27 (son of #2 above) (T VA T), Martha 25, Elizabeth 46 (sis)
4. SKILES, George 42, Margaret 38, Margaret 11, George 9, Jacob 7 (broken arm), Susanna 5, Joseph 3, Isabelle 1
5. SKILES, Ephraim 40 (T VA T), Mary A. 30, Eliza J. 7, Elizabeth 4, Rutha 2
6. SMITH, Henry 59 (T NC T), America 35 (wife) (T NC NC), Dow 5 (son), Sistira 3 (dau), James 2, Mary 20 (dau), Sophena 2 (g dau), Monroe 3/12 (b. Jan) (g son)
7. SMITH, Henry C. 26, Elizabeth 26, Isaac 5, John H. 4, George W. 2
8. SMITH, Isaac 57 (T NC T), Hannah 60, Rutha J. 35, Tempa 30, Tempa 13 (g dau), Margaret A. 7 (g dau), Nancy P. 6 (g dau), Henry 2 (g son)

Page 16, Dist. 8

1. MILLER, Sophia 46 (widow) (MO T T), Mary 14 (T T MO), Hannah 13, Jane 8, Rebecca 7
2. SMITH, William 33, Melinda 25 (AL T AL), John 8, William J. 5, Martha 2, Joseph 6/12 (b. Nov)
3. STRANAHAN, Charles C. 71 (NY CT CT), Margaret E. 61, Alice L. 29, Ira H. 23, Ansel A. 20, Charles E. 18
4. ROBERSON, Isaac 76 (KY KY NC)
5. DODSON, John 65
6. BEAVERT, Sarah 70
7. ROGERS, Ida 22 (asst in college)

Page 17, Dist. 9

1. SKILES, John 50, Ruth 54, Rebecca 21, Susanna 20
2. PATTON, William 20 (AL T T), Elizabeth 20, William 1
3. SMITH, William 58 (T NC T), Elizabeth 62, Elvira 38, Mary E. 14 (g dau)
4. BOWMAN, Henry 50, Rebecca 45 (T T KY), William 21, Delpha A. 18, Mary C. 15, Lewis 14, Samuel 9, Margaret 6, Emma 4
5. McWILLIAMS, Daniel 50 (T T NC), Maryann 47, John 28, Margaret 21, Alfred 13, Rebecca 9, Emma 7
6. HIXSON, Josiah 32, Elizabeth 30 (T VA VA), ___ R. 8 (son), John W. 10, Pleasant 4, Robert S. 2, Anderson 6/12 (b. Nov)
7. STEWART, Robert 36, Ruth 29, James 8
8. STEWART, Delila 63 (widow), Elizabeth 45 (sis), Nancy 13 (g dau)
9. GRAHAM, William 30, Samantha E. 25, Sarah E. 8, Samuel W. 7, Letta K. 4, Mary E. 1, Sis 1/12 (b. May)

Hh#	Page 18, Dist. 9

1. HIXSON, John M. 27, Eliza 17 (wife), Minna E. 4/12 (b. Jan); STEWART, John E. 22 (laborer); MILLER, Lincoln 18 (laborer)
2. HATFIELD, Sarah 26, Mary E. 8/12 (b. Sep); FURGERSON, Clarissa 17 (boarder)
3. HIXSON, Eliza C. 62 (widow) (T ___)
4. HIXSON, Joseph S. 25 (son of #3) (T NC VA), John P. 16 (servant) (B)
5. HIXSON, Tennessee (B) 31, Sally 6 (dau), Dove 4 (dau)
6. HIXSON, George W. 49, Temperance 44, Francis A. 18, Milla J. 16, George W. 13, Nancy A. 9, Ruth E. 6, Martin L. 11/12 (b. Jun)
7. WELCH, John 26, Letta 22, Lucy A. 4, Nancy 2, COWAN, Harrison 56 (hireling)
8. POPE, Jerome A. 21, Margaret 30 (sis), Elija M. 23 (bro), Charlie 20 (bro)
9. HUGHES, Temperance 68 (T NC NC)
10. HUGHS, Jerry (B) 34, Louisa 34, Josie 10, Virginia 8, James 7, Jesse 6, Eliza 4, George 2
11. HUGHS, George W. (B) 32, Laura 26, Savanna 10, Emeline 7, Samuel 6, Elijah 3, Eddie 2
12. HUGHS, James R. (B) 22, Florence 20 (NC T T)

Page 19, Dist. 9

1. JOHNSON, Daniel 38, Eliza 39, Elizabeth 21 (this name crossed out on schedule), Martha 13 (rheumatism), Jane 12 (rheumatism), Daniel 10, Arvee 6 (son) (rheumatism), Tate 2 (son)
2. MILLER, Southward 20, Elizabeth 18
3. MILLER, John 21, Mary 23, John 2
4. HORN, John 84 (T MD MD), Leannah 64 (wife) (insane); SKILES, John 1 (g son), John 16 (g nephew)
5. CLEMENT, Nancy 51 (widow), Jefferson 25, Ailsey 17 (dau), George 14
6. SMITH, Lewis 24 (blacksmith), Nancy E. 19, James R. 2, Fleming J. 7/12 (b. Oct)
7. STEWART, John 41; SMITH, Mary 40 (woman) (this couple not married), John 18, Sarah E. 16, Daniel 13, Jordan 10, Minerva 7, Horace M. 5, Trewhitt 5, Columbus 2
8. SMITH, Elizabeth 38, Uless 5 (son), Ella J. 2 (dau)
9. HIXSON, Samuel 29, Sarah 22, Newton 18 (relationship omitted), Jefferson 2/12 (b. Mar) (relationship omitted)
10. SMITH, William J. 33 (T VA T), Mary 30, Ida 10, Keziah 8 (dau), Nancy 8, Sterling

Page 20, Dist. 9

1. ROBERSON, Henderson (B) 28 (T T GA), Minerva 29 (T VA T), Jesse 8
2. LAMB, Bartley J. (B) 42, Emily 28 (wife) (VA VA VA), Mary 12 (fever), John 10, Sarah 8, Martha 7, James 4, Hester 2, Minta 5/12 (b. Feb)
3. AUSTIN, William 23 (T VA VA), Jane 25 (GA SC SC), James 1
4. ROBERSON, Moses (B) 23, Nancy 32 (sis), Houston 18 (nephew), Fanny 14 (niece), Dora 2 (niece)
5. ESTES, Samuel C. 21 (GA SC SC), Kizziah 22, William C. 3, Samuel C. 1 (AL)
6. HIXSON, John B. 37, Letty 37 (T GA T), John W. 13, George 12, Mary Ann 10, Rachel E. 3
7. GRAHAM, John 35 (T GA T), Margaret 27, James H. 6, Easter E. 5, Mary A. 3, Isabel 1
8. HIXSON, James L. 41, Eveline 40, Mary E. 15, Daughter 2 (AL)
9. HIXSON, John M. 49, Rutha J. 74 (mother)
10. HIXSON, Ruben 61 (farmer & blacksmith), Maryann 53 (T T NC), Timothy 21, Anderson 18, James F. 15

Hh#   Page 21, Dist. 9

1. HIXSON, Andrew (B) 54, Kumiles 32 (wife),
       Elias A. 16 (AL), Delila 13, James 12,
       Sarah 9, William 7, George 7
2. SMITH, James 56 (VA VA VA), Esther 42 (wife)
       (T T GA), Mary 20 (T VA VA), James M.
       17 (T VA T), Sarah M. 12 (T VA T)
3. HURD, George 22, Eliza 20, Eva E. 2 (AL),
       JamesL. 2/12 (b. Mar) (T)
4. HENDON, Robert 19 (T AL T), Susan 22, Sarah
       2
5. HIXSON, James M. 52, Susanna 50 (T VA T),
       Houston 24, Mary J. 22, Daily 19 (son),
       Fanny 15
6. SKILES, Rebecca 49, Martha J. 22 (dau),
       William 17 (son), James 13 (son),
       Mary E. 8 (dau), John B. 1 (g son)
7. SMITH, Madison 30, Margaret 28, Sophrona
       9, Audley 6 (son), John 4
8. HIXSON, William 82 (T MD T), Jane 40 (wife),
       John 2 (son), William 11/12 (b. Jun)
9. SMITH, John 45, Nancy 48 (sis), Elizabeth 45
       (sis), Mary E. 13 (niece), Emma J. 9
       (niece)
10. JOHNSON, Susan 58 (widow) (T VA VA), Palmer
       18, Sarah A. 11

                Page 22, Dist. 9

1. SMITH, Lafayettes 30, Elizabeth 29, James
       10, Nancy 5, Eliza 2
2. JOHNSON, Francis A. 24 (T T VA), Mary 21,
       James B. 1
3. HENSON, Alexander (B) 23, Alfred 31 (bro),
       Elizabeth 30 (sis)
4. HENSON, John (B) 32, Maryann 21 (wife),
       George 2, Caswell 3/12 (b. Mar)
5. GRAHAM, John 70 (GA NC NC), Mary E. 48
       (wife)
6. GRAHAM, Matison 28 (farmer & trader) (T GA
       T), Jennie 27, Julian 8, Matilda 5,
       James L. 3, Luther 5/12 (b. Dec);
       SMITH, Matilda 26 (boarder), Rufus 5,
       Christa 2, Willis 1/12 (b. Apr)
       (relationship of last 3 not given)
7. LAMB, Aaron B. 26, Nancy A. 27, Charles E. 4,
       James H. 2, Frances A. 8/12 (b. Sep)
8. SPRING, Reagan (B) 25, Parthena 23, Sarah J.
       1
9. BOWMAN, Daniel A. 50, Martha 47, Andrew J.
       25, John M. 23, Daniel A. 17, James T.?
       14, Benjamin R. 12, George W. 2
       (this name crossed off schedule), Mary
       H. 10, Phebe A. 6
10. BOWMAN, Andrew J. 47, Sarah 45, Sophrona 38
       (sis in law) (widow), Mary E. 20
       (niece), Phebe 68 (mother) (T NC NC)

                Page 23, Dist. 9

1. BOWMAN, Susan 38, Nancy 70 (mother) (T T NC)
2. SHANNON, Amanda 34 (widow), Anna 28, Melinda
       14, Eliza 8, James 7, Mary 5, Phebe
       2/12 (b. Mar) (g dau)
3. SHANNON, Pleasant 29, Nancy 29, Henly 14
       (son), Nancy E. 11, Elizabeth 9,
       Amanda 7, Martha 2
4. GILBREATH, Levander 51, Sarah E. 46 (wife)
       (GA T T), Sarah E. 5 (AL)
5. TETERS, James L. 34, Margaret V. 35 (T VA T),
       John L. 12, George W. 10, Liddia 8,
       Ida 6, Elva 3, Terry 1 (son)
6. BOYD, John T. 30, Mary 24, Edgar T. 1
7. LAMB, Alexander 34, Salena J. 28, Josie 4,
       Sally 1
8. LAMB, Margaret 52 (widow), Elizabeth 35
       (dau)
9. LEWIS, Thomas D. 62 (farmer & tanner) (T T
       VA), Rachel S. 53 (T NC VA), James B.
       19, Thomas A. 16
10. AUSTIN, Elijah F. 64, Phebe 60 (T T NC),
       Joseph B. 36, James H. 25, John B. 22,
       Joel B. 21, John L. 18; APPERSON,
       Elizabeth 43 (T VA VA)

Hh#   Page 24, Dist. 9

1. STANDIFER, Carrol 27, Elba F. 21, Joseph B.
       3, Rachel D. 2
2. HATFIELD, Joseph 25, Louisa J. 38 (wife) (T
       NC VA),Lucy C. 16
3. STANDIFER, James E. 29, Martha 22, Florence 2,
       Alexander 4/12 (b. Jan)
4. DAVIS, William 38, Nancy 42, John 20, Caroline
       18, Thomas 13, Samuel 10, Lucy 4;
       HANEY, Rosa 67 (mother in law) (T VA VA)
5. AUSTIN, James W. 66 (VA VA VA), Susan 62 (T
       PA NC), Joel 27 (son) (incompetent--
       fits & insane) (T VA VA)
6. AUSTIN, Thomas 37 (T VA T), Purliney 29, John
       17 (son), Benjamin 15, Ellen 7, Oscar
       10/12 (b. Jul)
7. ONEAL, George W. 18 (T KY T), Frances 19,
       Aiter J. 11/12 (b. Jun)
8. CLEMENT, John 61 (T NC NC), Elizabeth 56 (SC
       SC GA), William R. 30, Araminta 25,
       Adam 15, Sally 11
9. MOORE, William A. 36 (merchant & miller),
       Minerva 34 (T NC NC); BROWN, Mary 44
       (sis in law) (T NC NC); HOGE, John 18
       (laborer)
10. DAVIS, Harrison 26, Sarah 27, Thomas 3, Mary
       6/12 (b. Nov)

                Page 25, Dist. 9

1. CAGLE, Henry 39, Rebecca A. 38, Phebe E. 18,
       William J. 14, Lenora J. 11, Elijah A.
       8, Henry L. 3
2. AUSTIN, Thomas J. 30, Sarah E. 30, James L. 9,
       Elijah F. 7, Frances A. 5, Opha S. 3
       (son)
3. HALE, Joseph L. 25 (T T NC), Lydia 33 (wife),
       Lucius F. 8, Byron E. 7, Charles M. 5,
       James D. 3, Thomas H. 2, Beulah 7/12
       (b. Oct)
4. HUGHES, Aaron 48, Penelope 41, Aaron D. 18,
       Hugh M. 16, Jesse L. 14, Penelope 11,
       Joseph A. 9, Martha 6, Ruben 3, Eliza-
       beth 1
5. HIXSON, William C. 53, Rachel 43 (rheumatism)
       (T NC NC), Ephraim 22, Samuel 19,
       William 18, James E. 17, Sally 13, Mar-
       garet A. 12, Wiley 9, Philip R. 7,
       Audley 4 (son), Jeremiah W. 1
6. LAMB, William 33 (T T VA), Sarah E. 35, Lethy
       9, Luvena E. 7, Sarah E. 4, William A.
       9/12 (b. Aug) (children's relationships
       not listed)

                Page 26, Dist. 9

1. HIXSON, John H. 33, Nancy E. 32 (T T NC),
       William J. 15, Sarah A. 12, Newton J.
       10, Frances E. 7, Thomas E. 5, Richard
       C. 2, Stephens 2/12 (b. Mar)
2. STANDIFER, Shelton C. 65 (T VA VA), Nancy 66
       (KY NC NC), Thomas A. 14 (g son)
3. STANDIFER, William C. 33 (T T VA), Elva J.
       32 (T VA VA), James L. 11, Joel C. 9,
       John H. 6, Alfred L. 11/12 (b. Jun)
4. HALE, James 54, Mary 65 (wife) (NC NC NC)
5. LAMB, Patrick D. 57 (T KY T), Elizabeth C.
       52, Lois S.? 31, Ruth D. 27, Fanando
       C. 22, Darius E. 20, Cyrus J. 17,
       Frances E. 17, Adolphus P. 15, Mary C.
       15, Hannibal B. 9, Louisa E. 6, Uffa H.
       3 (son)
6. JONES, James 32, Adeline 35 (T VA VA), Adeline
       35 (T VA VA), James 10, George 9, Kiziah
       7 (dau), Reilly S. 5, Martha E. 4, Mary
       J. 2
7. LAMB, Eliza J. 54 (widow) (VA VA VA), James
       M. 30 (T VA T), Adam C. 24, Mary M. 15,
       HICKENBOTTOM, Aaron A. 6 (nephew) (T T
       VA)
8. JOHNSON, James B. 22 (T VA T), Mary J. 19
9. DAVIS, William M. 64 (T VA NC), Lucius F. 6
       (son)

Hh#   Page 27, Dist. 9

1. SMITH, William H. 26, Eliza E. 24 (T T VA),
        Aaron D. 4, Crosia 2 (dau), Dosia (b.
        May)
2. JOHNSON, Fraces (sic) A. 54 (widow) (VA VA
        VA), Willie M. 20 (son) (T T VA),
        Lucius E. 17 (son)
3. HAZZARD, John N. 40, Mary E. 36 (T NC T),
        William M. 13, John C. 11 (KY), James
        D. 7 (KY), Martha C. 5 (T), Mary E.
        3, Daniel C. 5/12 (b. Jan)
4. DAVIS, William S. 40 (T VA T), Elizabeth 31,
        Gilbert 13, Sally 11, Minna 8, Mary 7,
        William 6, James 4, Cuba 8/12 (b.
        Sep) (dau)
5. BEAVERT, Thomas 26 (T GA GA), Frances 21,
        William 2, Mary 6/12 (b. Nov)
6. HUGHS, Cornelius 21, Nancy J. 17 (wife), John
        M. 3/12 (b. Feb)
7. CLARK, Jonas 61, Mary 56, Anna J. 20, Joseph
        19, Charles 15 (fever), Ida 11
8. GATES, John T. 50 (T T VA), Eliza J. 40 (T
        NC GA), Puloulto 20 (son), Barzilla
        18 (dau), Stanton B. 16, Erby S. 14,
        Pamelia S. 10, Z. 6 (dau)
9. LAMB, Patrick 27 (T T VA), Lucy L. 12 (T T
        KY), Mary L. 5

                    Page 28, Dist. 9

1. LAMB, Euclid H. 25, Martha 25
2. HATFIELD, James 30, Nancy A. 33 (T T VA),
        Savanna 9, Luella 7, Lois 5, Julia 2,
        Nancy (b. May)
3. LAMB, Aaron B. 32, Margaret L. 23, Girtie 6,
        Mary E. 5, Stokely D. 2; REED, Fanny
        19 (a home)
4. POPE, Levander 31, Martha A. 27, Henry 11
        (son), Josie 7, Attie 8 (dau), Charlie
        6 (TX), James J. (TX)
5. GREER, Isah S. 66 (SC SC SC), Anna 64,
        Laura A. 24, Jonas C. 22
6. RAINS, Levander 26, Josie 24, Luther S. 3,
        Arthur 4/12 (b. Nov)
7. WRIGHT, Joseph E. 30 (GA NC GA), Elizabeth
        R. 19 (wife), Lovado 7/12 (b. Oct)
        (dau)
8. BOYD, Elliott H. 35, Mary C. 32
9. MARTIN, Telitha 48 (widow), William 19, David
        16, Martha 12; BRITT, James 15 (nephew)
        Susan 20 (niece), Martha 3 (g niece),
        John 1 (g nephew)

INDEX

The index applies to this booklet only. It includes
the names of all heads of household plus individuals
whose surnames differed from that of the head of
household. The name is followed by the person's age,
the booklet page number and then the household number
as it appears on the original schedules.

ABLE, William 32, 12-16
ACUFF, J. H. 35, 10-168
    J. S. 38, 9-148
    James 33, 2-89
    Jonathan 71, 2-88
    William 61, 12-36
AGEE, Hortense 4, 11-2
    Margarett 6, 11-2
    Martha 36, 11-2
    Nancey 2, 11-2
    Nicholas 35, 11-2
    Samuel 59, 12-49
    Thomas 36, 4-202
    Victorine 8, 11-2
    William 39, 6-271
AIKIN, Posey 35, 4-189
ALDRICH, Ellen C. 15, 2-92
    Emma 14, 2-92
ALEXANDER, Sarah B. 60, 17-4
    Stephen H. 58, 16-9
    William 29, 17-6
ALLEN, John 82, 15-202
ANDERSON, Audly 75, 13-87
    James 25, 13-61
    James F. 33, 17-5
    Louiza 35, 1-19
    W. A. 41, 17-3
ANGEL, Jackson 52, 3-121
    William 48, 3-124
ANGLE, Elizabeth 40, 13-96
ANNIS, John 28, 12-18
APPERSON, Elizabeth 43, 20-10
ATCHLEY, G. W. 54, 10-169
    J. W. M. 25, 10-170
    James 25, 9-129
AULT, George W. 31, 5-237
    William H. 23, 6-273
AUSTIN, Eley 28, 13-88
    Elijah F. 64, 20-10
    James 73, 13-88
    James W. 66, 20-5
    Thomas 37, 20-6
    Thomas J. 30, 20-2
    William 23, 19-3
BAGGETT, Drura B. 50, 2-67
BAIN, John 60, 12-44
BALLARD, Joseph G. 33, 5-209
BARBER, Edward 61, 12-15
    James E. 1, 3-142
    Sarah B. 27, 3-142
    William 22, 12-52
BARGER, Hugh 31, 19-5
    William T. 35, 18-1
BARNETT, James 38?, 11-6
BATES, Henry 46, 16-8
BEACH, John 6, 3-130
    Mary 29, 12-53
    Oliver C. 67, 2-107
    Sampson L. 28, 2-100
BEAN, John W. 45, 18-4
BEAVERT, Sarah 70, 19-6
    Thomas 26, 21-5
BEDWELL, Andrew J. 50, 3-108
    Martha 78, 2-80
BELL, Clarissa 37, 15-171
    David R. 42, 15-200
BENNET, Roscow 24, 16-217
BENNETT, Hosy 50, 14-117
BILLBERY, Chamberlain 53, 10-189
    Henry 28, 10-188
BILLINGSLEY, A. B. 66, 9-117
    Ach 68, 9-121
    Anderson 48, 9-137
    Fanny 30, 15-202
    J. T. 29, 8-91
    Jane R. 66, 9-144
    L. T. 37, 9-143
    Martin 45, 9-138
    Nute 50, 9-119
BIRCH, Mahaly 60, 14-125
BIRDITT, Harritt 27, 7-35
    R. E. 13, 7-35
    Samuel 47, 7-27
    Thomas 44, 8-50
BLACKBURN, Cesel 23, 13-88
    Robert G. 47, 4-155
BLANKINSHIP, Gilford G. 40, 2-94
BLAYLOCK, Frances J. 57, 4-170

BLAYLOCK, Isaac 2, 1-26
    Jesse 30, 4-171
    Richard 63, 4-164
    Thomas F. 37, 4-166
    William A. 28, 3-133
BLEVINS, Esquire 17, 15-203
    Joseph 27, 15-192
    Samuel 48, 16-7
    Squire 65, 1-16
    William 20, 14-142
BLODGETT, Louisa M. 48, 4-188
BLUFF, Dolly 11, 5-237
BOLTON, James 24, 15-197
    Lana 60, 14-126
BOMAN, David 52, 15-201
BORING, J. D. 18, 9-135
    J. H. 60, 9-133
    John 27, 12-24
    P. H. 19, 9-134
BOSTON, George W. 23, 5-226
    William C. 39, 5-215
BOWLIN, Edmund 75, 18-3
    Lynda 38, 18-1
    Orlean 41, 18-9
BOWMAN, Andrew J. 47, 20-10
    Afred M. 20, 18-4
    Daniel A. 50, 20-9
    Ellis H. 50, 18-7
    Henry 50, 19-4
    Isaac 27, 18-2
    John R. 27, 18-8
    Susan 38, 20-1
    William T. 22, 18-3
BOYD, Benjaman F. 33, 17-2
    Byron B. 4, 18-2
    Elliott H. 35, 21-8
    George W. 40, 17-6
    John L. 26, 12-37
    John T. 30, 20-6
    Josie F. 9, 18-6
    Julia 26, 18-2
    Lafayette 30, 12-38
    Right H. 26, 17-4
    S. W. 63, 8-97
    William 40, 11-9
    William J. 59, 17-5
BOYNTON, Lewis 43, 4-172
BRANNON, Damon 24, 12-26
BRANNUM, William 34, 19-6
BREWER, Elizabeth 77, 4-191
    Elizabeth 59, 4-186
    Pleasant A. 21, 4-187
    Pleasant B. 30, 4-190
BRIDGEMAN, William 30, 13-91
BRIDGMAN, Alex 35, 12-29
    Alex 35, 10-193
    Anthony 60, 13-104
    Don 25, 12-14
    Edward 46, 14-123
    Essix 30, 13-69
    George 44, 13-62
    Guseman 13, 15-164
    Jack 38, 12-54
    Jack 50, 13-106
    John 11, 12-36
    Mariah 52, 15-167
    Neoma 37, 12-13
    Oliver 24, 7-10
    Oliver 22, 6-268
    Richard 35, 14-149
    Samuel 36, 2-78
    Tilda 27, 13-105
BRITT, George 19, 18-2
    James 15, 21-9
    John 1, 21-9
    Martha 3, 21-9
    Susan 20, 21-9
BROCK, D. H. 62, 16-3
    Elihu 53, 13-76
    James 21, 13-101
    Jesse 58, 1-32
    John 21, 17-4
    Wm. 60, 9-127
    William 27, 13-102
    William A. 24, 6-279
BROWDER, Alex 17, 13-65
    Alexander 23, 13-99
BROWN, B. J. 45, 10-176

BROWN, B. J. 13, 10-176
    C. C. 25, 7-42
    Carter 24, 12-17
    Elijah 42, 13-77
    Elisha 44, 11-236
    Emiline 35, 7-2
    J. C. sr. 24, 7-33
    J. R. 59, 7-32
    Jackson 35, 12-30
    Jas. M. 56, 8-62
    John T. 38, 7-299
    Joseph 36, 18-8
    L. 50, 10-176
    Lucy 25, 11-221
    Martha 2, 11-221
    Mary 44, 20-9
    Mary 75, 10-176
    Mary E. 16, 10-176
    R. W. 37, 7-35
    Reuben H. 46, 5-208
    Robert 40, 8-51
    Sarah 56, 8-75
    Sarah 82, 13-77
    T. O. 45, 8-54
    Thomas 30, 8-77
    William A. 34, 12-22
BRUCE, Joseph E. 21, 6-249
BURCH, Franklin 41, 14-157
BURNETT, Daniel 27, 6-274
    Nicholas 57, 15-175
    William 55, 5-229
BUTLER, John W. 51, 17-3
CAFFS, Lizzie 19, 8-60
CAGLE, Henry 39, 20-1
    Littleton 27, 1-24
CAMPBELL, Eli 23, 16-245
    Obediah 29, 15-180
CAMPBELLE, John 25, 18-9
CAPPS, Margaret S. 12, 6-274
CARD, Bird 46, 12-46
CARR, Daniel 42, 11-8
    William 88, 18-4
CARROLL, Lewis 17, 17-4
CARSON, Rheubin 33, 18-5
CARTER, Charles 28, 8-87
CARTRIGHT, Henry 34, 8-53
    Semon 35, 5-243
    William 71, 4-199
CASTELLER, Micheil 20, 15-166
CAVILLE, T. C. 12, 7-37
CHILDERS, Adaline 56, 2-75
    Alexanders 28, 13-92
    Andrew 40, 15-206
    John A. 21, 2-72
    Mary 34, 3-146
CHILDRESS, Joseph M. 26, 2-64
CHILDS, John T. 30, 10-197
CHRISTIAN, Christopher 80, 12-43
CLARK, Daniel 65, 10-185
    Francis M. 52, 4-177
    Gilbert 50, 7-9
    J. J. 54, 11-245
    Jacob 51, 7-22
    John? 20, 9-111
    John A. 28, 7-41
    Jonas 61, 21-7
    Mary 15, 1-16
    Nancy 39, 11-245
    Samuel 25, 7-39
    Susanne 34, 1-16
    Thomas 17, 7-292
    W. B. 55, 9-123
    William 30, 13-82
CLAYTON, Nancy 57, 9-107
CLEMENT, John 61, 20-8
    Nancy 51, 19-5
CLIFTON, Sally 31, 18-9
CLOSE, Nancy 50, 6-281
COFFMAN, M. 23, 9-140
    T. J. 52, 10-186
COLBERT, Carroll 7, 12-54
    Sarah 16, 12-54
COLLINS, William J. 7, 3-138
    Zachary T. 10, 3-139
COLVARD, Sarah 45, 2-63
    Wiley M. 45, 2-77
COMLEY, Etta 21, 12-27
CONLEY, John W. 31, 16-236

COOK, Chany C. 75, 4-201
    Lucien 71, 15-204
COOLEY, Jesse 32, 18-7
    Philip 38, 18-4
COOPER, John 45, 14-130
COWAN, Harrison 56, 19-7
COX, J. M. 47, 9-125
    John W. 31, 1-35
    Marion 35, 10-182
CRAVENS, Sarah F. 65, 17-1
CRAWFORD, Jonathan H. 42, 4-161
    Mary 45, 4-162
CREASON, Jasper 35, 3-126
    William 64, 4-156
CREECH, Benedict 25, 1-18
    Richard 79, 1-15
CROCKET, William 25, 7-24
CUMMINGS, Rosa 46, 13-63
CUNNINGHAM, C. O. 30, 9-149
CURTIS, Cathorine 38, 12-43
    H. 22, 10-181
    Hezekiah 69, 13-103
    Levander 28, 10-179
DANIEL, Robert 57, 13-80
    Syrus 26, 14-145
DAVIS, Harrison 26, 20-10
    William 38, 20-4
    William M. 64, 20-9
    William S. 40, 21-4
DAY, Hattie 4, 18-1
    Jesse F. 33, 5-246
    Mary 25, 18-1
    William 27, 6-248
DE BORD, Abijah 24, 2-82
    John W. 50, 2-73
    Martin 23, 2-83
    Mary 62, 2-81
DENNIS, Isham 48, 18-3
DILL, Joseph 12, 1-42
    Newton 15, 17-5
DODSON, John 65, 19-5
DOTSON, Jack 54, 10-172
DOUGLAS, John 50, 1-26
    Missouri 45, 1-25
DUGGER, Terressa 40, 12-12
DUKE, Benjamin A. 54, 1-5
    Matilda 7, 1-21
    Melinda 50, 1-30
DUN, Susan 57, 11-213
DURHAM, Lucinda 36, 15-174
    Sarah 39, 13-86
DYE, James 33, 17-5
    Obediah 45, 17-7
    Perry 38, 17-8
    Perry 22, 18-4
DYRE, J. C. 23, 7-6
    James 38, 10-200
    John M. 3, 11-222
    Samuel 21, 7-7
    Sintha 22, 11-222
    Will 38, 9-124
EDMONDS, John R. 26, 4-193
    Jordan 54, 4-196
ELLERSON, Melvina 58, 12-45
ERVIN, N. P. 9, 3-142
ERWIN, Harvy 52, 9-126
ESSEX, Elizabeth 20, 11-7
ESTES, Samuel C. 21, 19-5
ETHERTON, John 65, 11-215
EVERETT, David 32, 15-184
FAMER, Samuel 36, 9-122
FARMER, Alexander F. 31, 3-143
    Aquilla 51, 15-166
    Martin 39, 10-178
    W. W. 44, 8-92
FERGERSON, Margarett 55, 16-216
FERGUSON, Charles 39, 1-14
    Elisha 33, 1-12
    William H. 36, 3-149
FLINN, Mary 20, 12-24
FLYNN, Mary E. 21, 2-60
    Rebecca A. 18, 2-60
FORD, Elizabeth A. 47, 17-1
    Ira 52, 2-61
FORLEY, J. J. 53, 16-5
    John 30, 16-6
    Patton 22, 16-8
    Thomas H. 24, 16-7

FOSTER, Ephraim H. 33, 5-219
    Joshua 26, 5-218
    Julia Ann 65, 4-163
    William 45, 8-73
    William 21, 15-169
FRADA, Elizabeth 18, 13-71
    Baxter W. 24, 2-97
    George McD. 20, 3-114
FRALEY, Johnathan 54, 14-109
FRANKLIN, Peter 63, 11-10
FRASIER, John 67, 3-117
    Saml. P. 39, 2-85
    William G. 21, 2-103
FREEMAN, Bird 50, 3-152
    James M. 38, 3-153
FREILEY, Mary W. 48, 5-232
FULLER, Dientha 87, 4-179
FURGERSON, Anna 14, 15-203
    Clarissa 17, 19-2
    Elizabeth 21, 12-43
    James 41, 15-170
    Mary 30, 14-140
    Mitt 60, 16-231
    Samuel 45, 11-7
GAD, Ansel 66, 18-1
    Jethro 53, 18-2
    John D. 36, 18-3
GAMBLE, William 52, 14-142
GANT, Daniel 38, 15-195
GATES, John T. 50, 21-8
GEARY, Hannah 55, 11-246
GENTRY, J. P. 35, 10-161
    John 65, 7-34
    Robert 26, 10-180
GIDDEON, Beckie 31, 11-219
GILBERT, Jessey 38, 11-7
GILBREATH, Levander 51, 20-4
GILL, John 40, 11-240
    Samuel P. 27, 9-142
GOINS, Isabella 26, 1-29
    Matilda 25, 1-28
    Rebecca 36, 1-27
GOTT, Lafayette 31, 5-244
    Russell 68, 5-245
GOURENS, Vaney A. 5, 17-9
    William 3, 17-9
GOWENS, Alfred 22, 18-6
    John 63, 18-5
GRAHAM, John 35, 19-7
    John 70, 20-5
    Matison 28, 20-6
    William 30, 19-9
    William R. 32, 4-160
GREEN, George 53, 16-223
    Sarah 41, 6-249
GREER, Alexander C. 31, 18-3
    Cilley 27, 12-33
    David 44, 4-179
    Henry 29, 15-159
    Henry C. 41, 12-48
    Isah S. 66, 21-5
    John 20, 14-112
    Martha 28, 12-22
    Mary 78, 14-144
    Moses 50, 14-137
    Moses 20, 6-265
    William H. 59, 14-138
GREGOREY, James 32, 16-221
GREGORY, Thomas 43, 16-238
GRIFFETH, Thomas J. 48, 2-65
GRIMSLEY, Abraham 59, 16-242
GRIMSLY, James M. 38, 16-243
GUESS, Richard 40, 5-233
HALE, Alfred 26, 6-260
    Aquilla 46, 7-294
    Burrell 35, 1-21
    Elisha 39, 8-83
    James 54, 20-4
    James 35, 8-59
    James A. 43, 8-82
    Jeremiah 70, 11-2
    Jesse H. 22, 6-258
    John 56, 8-99
    John 50, 1-20
    John I. 22, 2-105
    John N. 65, 8-81
    John P. 38, 12-26
    John R. 32, 6-261

HALE, Joseph L. 25, 20-3
    Martin 27, 9-100
    Richard 65, 15-213
    S. S. 32, 9-102
    Sallie 65, 8-98
    Sarah 19, 4-180
    T. F. 36, 8-93
    Thomas 37, 8-58
    Thomas 69, 9-101
    Thomas S. 31, 4-157
    W. C. 37, 9-103
    W. H. 39, 11-221
    William 67, 6-259
    William 26, 1-50
HALEY, John B. 36, 5-238
    Peter 28, 5-228
HALL, Cintha 60, 15-173
    Eliza 50, 12-35
    Eva 22, 12-35
    Ferrell 40, 16-226
    Jacob 26, 9-150
    Jessey 42, 12-28
    John 69, 17-3
    Thomas 46, 14-136
    William 50, 19-8
HAMFILTON, John 29, 7-29
HAMILTON, Isaac 6-270
    John 60, 6-264
HAMPILTON, Mary 79, 9-109
HANEY, Rosa 67, 20-4
HANKINS, James 1, 8-69
HARDIN, Nancy 36, 4-200
HART, Charles 36, 13-88
    Henry W. 43, 12-24
HARVEY, James C. 52, 2-66
HARWOOD, Benj. 38, 16-227
HASKEW, Adam V. B. 44, 1-6
    Brown 19, 14-132
    Hezekiah 21, 14-132
    Mary 40, 17-8
    Samuel T. 16, 17-9
    William 19, 15-203
    William 68, 17-7
HATFIELD, James 30, 21-2
    Joseph 25, 20-2
    Margaret J. 4, 18-2
    Robert B. 20, 18-6
    Sarah 26, 19-2
    Taylor 36, 18-3
HAVEY, Margaret 16, 16-246
HAWKINS, John 64, 8-80
    Pinkney 23, 15-191
HAYES, Aaron 16, 5-234
    Henry 10, 5-234
HAZZARD, John N. 40, 21-3
HEARD, James C. 40, 17-10
    John 59, 12-43
HEDGLEY, William 36, 15-166
HEMPHILL, Samuel C. 57, 2-92
HENDERSON, Anne 51, 10-166
    Bird 40, 11-239
    Frank 44, 11-235
    Jas. 87, 11-234
    Jasper 37, 11-233
    John E. 4, 10-203
    Mary 23, 10-203
    R. M. 47, 11-230
    T. F. 32, 7-40
HENDON, Robert 19, 20-4
HENNIGAR, Marcus O. 33, 15-172
HENNIGER, F. A. 59, 17-2
HENRY, Alfred 32, 12-27
    Frank 27, 12-24
    James 37, 14-143
    John W. 47, 16-219
    Milton 22, 13-64
HENSON, Alexander 23, 20-3
    Elbert 26, 13-95
    Erastus 25, 13-65
    John 32, 20-4
    Lafayette 19, 16-1
    Samuel 36, 12-40
    William 38, 13-66
HICKEMBOTTOM, Celia 55, 1-36
HICKENBOTTOM, Aaron A. 6, 20-7
    William B. 18, 1-51
HICKENBOTTON, John 23, 17-6
HICKMAN, Mary L. 16, 5-217

HICKMAN, Nancy J. 17, 5-217
HILL, John W. 12, 3-128
HINCH, John C. 46, 5-226
HINES, John 70, 9-105
HITCHCOCK, James 70, 1-48
    James D. 25, 1-49
    Wilburn 23, 1-44
HIXON, Allen 18, 16-225
    Fountain 15, 14-149
HIXSON, Andrew 54, 20-1
    Eliza C. 62, 19-3
    George W. 49, 19-6
    James L. 41, 19-8
    James M. 52, 20-5
    John B. 37, 19-6
    John H. 33, 20-1
    John M. 49, 19-9
    John M. 27, 19-1
    Joseph S. 25, 19-4
    Josiah 32, 19-6
    Ruben 61, 19-10
    Samuel 29, 19-9
    Tennessee 31, 19-5
    Thomas J. 28, 18-1
    William 82, 20-8
    William C. 53, 20-5
HOGE, John 18, 20-9
    Nathaniel 32, 9-118
    Preston 44, 7-23
HOGUE, James L. 50, 13-93
HOLLAND, David 25, 1-41
    David 55, 1-51
    Joseph 24, 1-55
    Kitty 23, 1-52
    Leroy 25, 17-2
    Robert 57, 1-42
    Thomas 29, 17-5
    William 43, 1-56
HOLLOWAY, William C. 52, 6-256
HOLT, Thomas 55, 10-171
HOPKINS, Isaac 64, 2-102
    Jesse M. 53, 3-119
    Margaret 53, 3-148
HORN, John 84, 19-4
HOUSTON, Delilah 77, 4-175
    James 30, 5-220
    William 38, 4-174
HOUTS, Henry 40, 13-83
HOWARD, Buckner 76, 18-8
    George W. 37, 18-5
    James J. 29, 17-3
    John 45, 11-7
    Mary 15, 15-199
    Reason D. 40, 18-6
HOXSON, Henninger 30, 18-10
HUDSON, Robert H. 65, 14-153
HUGHES, Aaron 48, 20-4
    Temperance 68, 19-9
HUGHS, Cornelius 21, 21-6
    George W. 32, 19-11
    James R. 22, 19-12
    Jerry 34, 19-10
HUMBLE, Andrew J. 24, 2-76
    Isaac 73, 16-232
    Lovina 46, 16-4
    Virginia 18, 16-4
    Wyatt 21, 16-4
HUNT, Lucinda 45, 18-4
HURD, George 22, 20-3
HUSE, Elizabeth 75, 11-231
HUSER, S. H. 1, 9-110
HUTCHESON, Cas. 25, 10-192
    Lee 26, 10-194
    M. 24, 8-49
    Malon 2, 7-42
    R. B. 40, 9-152
    Reuben 50, 10-159
    W. A. 43, 8-60
HUTCHISON, F. J. 50, 8-94
    J. T.? 46, 8-85
    Lucy 46, 8-88
    M. P. jr. 22, 8-86
    P. S. 68, 8-84
HYDER, Alfred 58, 5-217
INGRAM, Mary 57, 15-182
IVANS, Joseph A. 29, 6-276
IVES, John 26, 10-174
IVEY, John 31, 14-115

JAMES, Anderson 25, 13-58
    Hezekiah S. 60, 18-4
    Malvina 44, 18-5
    Samuel 19, 13-58
    Tandy 39, 18-10
    Willis 78, 3-152
JENINO, Carwell 48, 7-26
JOHNSON, C. 8, 11-245
    Crocket 51, 11-246
    Daniel 38, 19-1
    Eliza 20, 11-246
    Eva 3, 7-38
    Fraces A. 54, 21-2
    Francis A. 24, 20-2
    Jackson 16, 11-246
    James 35, 1-40
    James 10, 11-246
    James B. 22, 20-8
    Jarott 12, 9-131
    John 23, 1-53
    Margret 30, 9-131
    P. C. 26, 9-132
    Susan 58, 20-10
    Thomas 45, 1-33
    Thomas 27, 18-9
    Warren 63, 1-17
    William 60, 1-45
    William J. 37, 1-43
JONES, Azleteen 27, 1-10
    Benjamin F. 21, 18-1
    Catherine 42, 13-84
    Franklin 25, 4-167
    James 32, 20-6
    L. W. 57, 9-146
    Sassafine 7, 5-217
    Thomas 45, 12-31
    William 15, 12-18
JORDAN, Emma 33, 11-217
    George W. 29, 18-9
    Martha J. 43, 16-2
    W. A. 36, 9-131
JORDON, Asa 104, 16-234
KEEDY, Jacob 58, 17-7
    Nancy 56, 15-185
    Virginia 69, 15-176
    William 29, 16-232
    Zachariah T. 31, 18-8
KEELER, Sarah 65, 11-5
KEENER, Jackson 55, 2-62
    Wayman 24, 15-177
    William 27, 2-58
KELLEY, James 36, 13-58
KING, Atrum T. 37, 16-224
    Jane 14, 1-28
    Jon. H. 46, 10-199
    Thomas 18, 1-28
KIZZIAH, George 29, 18-7
KNIGHT, Andrew C. 28, 2-91
    Elizabeth 75, 3-114
    Florence 11, 12-34
    Franklin M. 36, 3-130
    Jane 69, 3-145
    Laura 12, 12-34
    Margaret 35, 11-11
    Martha 16, 12-34
    Nancy 65, 12-34
    William 42, 6-286
LAMB, Aaron B. 32, 21-3
    Aaron B. 26, 20-7
    Alexander 34, 20-7
    Bartley J. 42, 19-2
    Eliza J. 54, 20-7
    Euclid H. 25, 21-1
    John K. 28, 17-6
    Margaret 52, 20-8
    Patrick 27, 21-9
    Patrick D. 57, 20-5
    William 33, 20-6
LANE, Gantt 35, 11-4
    Maggie J. 5, 6-279
LARRENCE, Whittenburg 13, 12-35
LAW, Delania 70, 10-206
LAWSON, David 48, 1-31
    Houston 29, 14-114
    J. A. 37, 10-160
    James 3, 1-11
    Jesse 50, 3-135
    Lyra 56, 14-156

LAWSON, Wesley 56, 3-134
LEA, Eliza Ann 52, 15-204
    Elizabeth 14, 11-4
    Emila 54, 14-150
    Louansa 64, 15-203
LEDBETTER, John 50, 1-2
LEE, Anderson 43, 6-287
    Benjamin F. 41, 6-275
    Harriet 40, 6-262
    T. A. 26, 8-62
    Thomas B. 23, 6-277
    William 45, 6-263
LEWIS, Dalton 20, 12-43
    Simon D. 45, 16-228
    Thomas D. 62, 20-9
LITTLE, F. M. 32, 7-25
    Francis M. 60, 5-242
LOCK, Maybell 15, 12-23
LOVELADY, James 45, 15-207
LOWERY, M. 35, 10-175
LOYD, Benjamin F. 43, 4-178
    Charles 40, 12-51
    Henry 25, 9-112
    Roland P. 53, 14-131
LOZA, John 20, 16-225
MANREY, John 5, 16-3
MARLER, Edgar 7, 18-6
MARSH, Terrell 30, 3-125
MARTIN, Absalom 60, 2-93
    James H. 26, 3-112
    Telitha 48, 21-9
MASON, Elizabeth 37, 3-118
    John A. 2, 3-118
MASSEY, James 18, 10-181
MASSY, Jennie 16, 7-35
    Robert 2, 15-185
MATHIS, Leander 44, 11-216
MATTHEWS, Mary 58, 15-184
MAYNARD, Fanny 45, 4-191
McCLAMEY, Jas. 30, 9-153
    R. H. 27, 7-43
McCLAMY, John 4, 9-104
    M. A. 22, 9-104
McCLELLEN, Mavia (Maria) 42, 7-8
McCLOUD, William 59, 14-113
McCULY, Thomas 45, 16-229
McDANIEL, Thomas 23, 15-162
    Tolbert 37, 16-239
McDONALD, James 26, 1-16
    William 49, 4-173
McDONOLD, John 38, 11-211
McDOWELL, Anna J. 16, 8-74
    J. C. 24, 7-3
    Jane 70, 8-64
    Luteshy? 53, 7-16
    W. B. 45, 8-66
    W. S. 55, 8-79
McGAN, Polk 26, 15-212
    Susan 56, 15-210
McGEE, Thomas 21, 7-11
McJUNKENS, Jack 52, 12-55
McJUNKIN, Margaret L. 16, 2-102
    Martha A. 51, 2-102
    Sherman C. 10, 2-102
    Thadeus T. 46, 2-102
    William S. 13, 2-102
McJUNKINS, Andrew 28, 16-222
    James 22, 12-24
McKINNIE, John 29, 11-241
McMILLON, Asbury 21, 7-297
    Joseph 51, 7-293
McPHERSON, M. 14, 9-105
McREYNOLD, Henry 50, 14-133
McREYNOLDS, Alexander 38, 13-98
    Alexander 54, 14-139
    Benj. 62, 1-3
    Henry 52, 1-1
    Isaac 34, 16-225
    Johnsey 57, 13-62
    Saml. M. 50, 15-171
    Samul 23, 13-70
    Wed. S. 26, 13-89
McWILLIAMS, Daniel 50, 19-5
MEDLEY, James 52, 2-95
MERCER, Peter 46, 9-139
MERRIMAN, Allen R. 46, 17-6
    Dianner 69, 16-2
    Lowry M. 35, 2-99

MERRITT, Scott 19, 13-102
MERSER, Forester 32, 11-7
    Mary 20, 11-7
MILLAKIN, Calvin 50, 11-237
    P. P. 23, 11-238
MILLARD, W. D. 21, 7-13
MILLER, Chalie E. 9/12, 8-79
    Eliza 37, 11-242
    John 21, 19-3
    Lincoln 18, 19-1
    Roland P. 22, 19-7
    Sallie 26, 8-79
    Sophia 46, 19-1
    Southward 20, 19-2
MILLS, F. J. 37, 11-224
    Levi 47, 11-223
MILTS, James 23, 16-221
MILUM, John A. 52, 2-98
MITCHELL, Gibs 45, 13-72
    Lue 15, 10-158
    Sallie 11, 10-158
MITTS, Andy 50, 11-228
    Nancy 55, 11-229
MOLES?, Henry 50, 10-176
MONTGOMERY, Jane R. 46, 8-48
    K. B. 32, 10-195
MOONEYHAM, Lucinda 56, 3-131
    Owen B. 38, 3-120
MOORE, James M. 21, 3-113
    Jesse 25, 15-215
    John 36, 3-147
    Nancy A. S. 24, 3-150
    Polly A. 49, 6-284
    Rachel V. 52, 3-122
    Sallie 16, 12-35
    William 65, 14-124
    William A. 36, 20-9
MORGAN, George W. 27, 5-224
    Thomas 32, 16-247
MORRIS, Drucilla C. 27, 4-194
MORSE, Charles H. 45, 2-96
MOYERS, Albert H. 35, 4-182
    Daisy I. 1, 4-185
    George A. 75, 4-183
    George A. 25, 4-198
    George L. 29, 4-184
MOZEN, John C. 31, 12-25
    Robert A. 36, 11-11
MULINEX, W. O. 32, 10-198
MUNAHAM, C. 48, 4-96
MURPHY, John B. 85, 17-3
NAIL, Elvira 65, 6-263
    Franklin 14, 6-270
    Margaret 51, 6-270
    Nelson 61, 14-129
NEAL, Jefferson 19, 13-58
    M. C. 34, 10-206
NEDD, Samuel 24, 10-173
NICKLES, Sallie 90, 8-75
NIDD, Jane 63, 10-191
NORTHRUP, S. J. 26, 10-177
    Solyman 48, 13-78
NORWOOD, Ada 19, 13-78
    Arthur 3/12, 13-78
    James 23, 13-78
    St. Clair 58, 11-1
ONEAL, George W. 18, 20-7
    Samuel 26, 17-10
ORME, Catherin 80, 14-144
    Wetherson 26, 14-144
ORMES, Charles 18, 5-235
OWENS, Mary 76, 16-230
    William 20, 14-136
OWINGS, Edward G. 65, 1-47
    Lu 44, 9-102
    W. M. 48, 9-110
PANKEY, Amelia C. 26, 3-120
    Charles 52, 10-187
    Mary 51, 10-195
PANKY, Alexander 10, 15-200
    Benjamin 30, 15-199
    Calvin 53, 12-39
PANTER, Alexander 47, 3-129
    Mary 72, 12-19
    Sampson 37, 12-20
PATTON, Elijah 42, 5-223
    F. T. 22, 10-190

PATTON, J. A. 44, 7-37
    Josiah 67, 6-254
    Martin 28, 6-255
    Owings 50, 10-162
    Thomas 32, 5-236
    William 20, 19-2
PAYME, John 25, 8-95
    N. P. 34, 9-151
PEARCE, Rachel 50, 11-245
PEARSON, Thomas D. 59, 3-144
PEMBERTON, Alfred 31, 16-6
    Constant 58, 1-9
PENDERGRASS, A. 28, 10-163
    Nancy 51, 11-244
    Wamey? 55, 10-165
PENNINGTON, Francis 22, 2-74
PERIN, S. E. 29, 16-2
PERRY, Oliver H. 29, 4-188
PHILIP, Richard 23, 14-119
PHILIPS, Elizabeth 48, 16-230
PIERCE, John 56, 18-10
PITTS, Charles 45, 13-106
POE, William 67, 3-151
POLLARD, I. N. 43, 9-141
PONSON?, Jack 26, 1-4
POPE, D. S. 34, 8-90
    J. T. 33, 17-6
    Jerome A. 21, 19-8
    Levander 31, 21-4
    Mary E. 37, 18-5
    Virginia T. 16, 18-5
    William 35, 11-3
PRATER, Darcus J. 9, 3-144
    Elizabeth 37, 4-159
PRICE, Delila 37, 16-5
    John 41, 16-4
PRITCHETT, James 57, 16-246
PULLEN, Agga 35, 5-213
PUTNAM, George V. 35, 1-7
    James M. 38, 1-13
    Mary 33, 1-8
RAINEY, Annie C. 50, 1-54
    Mary A. 54, 17-8
RAINS, Levander 26, 21-6
    Mahala 49, 17-1
    Marlen 57, 17-3
RANDALS, T. A. 34, 9-130
RANEY, Nancy 55, 15-165
    Nancy 55, 17-6
RANKEN, Amanda 40, 11-6
RANKIN, Alfred 33, 9-120
    D. F. 29, 10-157
    Dovie? 41, 10-158
    HEnry 30, 5-207
READ, Kezziah 45, 15-211
REAL, Charles 47, 16-4
    George W. 28, 19-9
    Peter 34, 19-1
    Solomon 26, 19-10
RECTOR, Jesse 22, 5-209
REED, Fanny 19, 21-3
    Margaret J. 25, 18-2
    Sarah F. 5, 18-2
REEDY, Henry 3, 15-171
    Nancy 29, 15-171
REESE, Dock 11, 12-34
RENFRO, George 54, 14-135
RICHARDS, Smith 23, 10-174
RICHARDSON, George 22, 13-81
    Leroy 31, 1-52
RICHEY, H. A. 57, 11-226
    James 27, 11-227
RIDLEY, Alaxander 56, 3-122
RIGSBEY, Gleam? 43, 12-41
    John 23, 12-47
    Lucinda 65, 13-60
RIGSBY, James 46, 14-141
    John 44, 14-110
    Plesant 23, 14-111
RITCHEY, David 30, 16-237
    Joseph 26, 16-241
ROBERSON, Adam 35, 15-181
    Henderson 28, 19-1
    Hezekiah 38, 12-35
    Inda 20, 12-19
    Isaac 76, 19-4
    James 44, 12-57

ROBERSON, James M. 64, 14-132
    Jane 40, 13-97
    Jeremiah 43, 14-152
    John R. 33, 15-179
    Matilda 41, 14-137
    Moses 23, 19-4
    Peter 41, 16-1
    Polk 35, 17-7
    Reuben 38, 13-67
    Tole 22, 12-20
    William 31, 15-178
    William 35, 15-198
ROBERTS, Hugh L. 50, 6-278
    Jas. L. 22, 11-212
    William W. 33, 7-298
RODDY, Newton T. 19, 5-226
ROGERS, Ida 22, 19-7
    Isaac 30, 7-5
    John 32, 16-2
    Keziah 64, 19-10
    Riley R. 52, 18-6
    William 28, 16-1
    William C. 48, 17-9
ROLANDS, Elvira 45, 11-225
ROLLINS, Daniel 52, 2-106
ROMINES, Henry 12, 9-152
ROSE, J. A. 40, 11-231
    Louiza 21, 5-238
    Lucindie 43, 7-19
    Nancy 18, 7-299
ROSS, James A. 43, 12-23
ROYAL, John 16, 18-1
ROYTON, Alice 40, 7-43
RUSSELL, Edmond 80, 16-233
    John 40, 2-57
    John J. 59, 1-46
RUTLEDGE, Benjamin 26, 15-168
    Jane 58, 15-183
    Lorenzo 27, 15-187
SAMPSON, John 55, 7-17
SAVAGE, Lucinda 60, 17-7
SCHOOLFIELD, Matthew 24, 14-127
    P. H. 54, 7-31
    Perry A. 40, 17-9
    Thomas 8, 15-199
    William 60, 13-68
SEALS, Charles A. 1, 17-9
    James 53, 3-142
    James 74, 3-132
    James Jn. 30, 3-140
    James T. 7, 3-145
    Sarah J. 48, 3-145
    Stacy A. 20, 17-9
    Zela 38, 3-141
SEGRAVES, Ben 42, 10-208
    J. F. R. 26, 10-156
    Jesse 37, 8-78
    Mary 59, 10-155
SELATHILL, Marsh 6, 7-25
SHAHERN?, J. B. 26, 7-36
SHANNON, Amanda 34, 20-2
    Pleasant 29, 20-3
    Thomas 28, 18-5
    Sally 11, 19-1
SHAW, Joseph 72, 11-232
SHOEMATE, Wm. 75, 9-106
SHUMATE, John 30, 14-121
    Margarett 33, 16-225
    Thomas 48, 14-122
SIMMONS, A. J. 39, 9-114
    Andrew 38, 3-138
SIMMONS, Belle S. 16, 3-135
    F. 20, 9-115
    J. P. 37, 9-116
    James 41, 3-139
    James R. 18, 3-142
    Jas. T. 48, 10-164
    John 65, 12-43
    John 50, 3-154
    Martha A. A. 11, 3-142
    Thomas 25, 3-118
    Thomas 19, 3-135
    William T. 40, 3-136
SIMPSON, Charles R. 6, 1-18
    Peter 39, 14-118
SINGLETON, Fanny 45, 4-158
    Thomas 8, 4-158

SKELLEM, Ida 7, 13-65
SKILES, Ephraim 40, 19-5
    George 42, 19-4
    Jacob 76, 19-2
    Jeferson 27, 19-3
    John 50, 19-1
    John 1, 19-4
    Joseph 24, 18-3
    Rebecca 49, 20-6
SKILLEM, James 30, 13-90
    James A. 41, 14-148
    Jesse 55, 14-155
    Nancy M. E. 27, 1-21
    Sarah 8, 15-167
    William 57, 14-154
SKILLERN, Alfred 63, 17-1
    Laura 20, 14-122
SLOAN, John H. 23, 5-244
SMITH, Arminta 13, 4-165
    Brook 54, 8-62
    Brooks jr. 6, 8-62
    Charlie 1, 8-62
    Christa 2, 20-6
    Columbus 2, 19-7
    D. C. 24, 8-62
    Daniel 13, 19-7
    Delila 15, 18-8
    Elizabeth 15, 16-2
    Elizabeth 38, 19-8
    Elizabeth 45, 4-165
    Elvia 16, 8-62
    Etheldridge 69, 4-165
    Frank 26, 8-61
    George W. 24, 2-70
    Henry 18, 17-7
    Henry 59, 19-6
    Henry C. 26, 19-7
    Horace M. 5, 19-7
    Isaac 57, 19-8
    Isaac 45, 17-5
    Isaac N. 37, 2-68
    Isaac N. 51, 18-2
    James 56, 20-2
    James 22, 9-145
    James H. 53, 4-199
    James M. 48, 3-127
    James M. 54, 2-69
    John 60, 18-7
    John 23, 19-11
    John 18, 19-7
    John 45, 20-9
    John 24, 2-84
    John G. 52, 2-80
    John H. 14, 8-62
    John P. 36, 4-169
    Jordan 10, 19-7
    Joseph 5, 18-4
    Julia 20, 13-58
    Lafayettes 30, 20-1
    Levander 4, 18-4
    Lewis 24, 19-6
    Luther 35, 7-15
    M. J. 62, 8-68
    Madison 30, 20-7
    Martha 30, 17-8
    Mary 40, 17-8
    Mary 40, 19-7
    Mary 26, 18-4
    Matilda 13, 15-177
    Matilda 26, 20-6
    Minerva 2, 18-4
    Minerva 7, 19-7
    Nancy 26, 18-8
    Noah 27, 2-71
    Patrick 19, 17-9
    Peter 48, 18-6
    Rachel 47, 16-3
    Rufus 5, 20-6
    Sally 13, 18-2
    Sarah 55, 16-2
    Sarah E. 16, 19-7
    Simon 4/12, 18-4
    T. F. 38, 8-67
    Timothy 13, 18-1
    Trewhitt 5, 19-7
    Vesta 3, 18-4
    William 58, 19-3
    Wm. 17, 9-128

SMITH, William 33, 19-2
    William 20, 8-70
    William 35, 18-9
    William B. 45, 4-168
    William H. 26, 21-1
    William J. 33, 19-10
    William Mc. 45, 17-9
    Willis, 1/12, 20-6
SNIDER, James D. 33, 2-59
SOLOMAN, Andrew 33, 13-79
SONGER, David 60, 1-39
    Frances 7, 2-58
SPEARMAN, Violet 17, 9-148
SPEARS, James 24, 16-238
    John 30, 16-244
    Peter 67, 12-32
    Taylor 28, 15-164
SPRING, Alexander 24, 14-120
    Benj. F. 62, 13-85
    George 40, 14-128
    James 42, 15-190
    Lucinda 60, 13-64
    Margaret 45, 11-3
    Martha 38, 15-163
    Reagan 25, 20-8
    Rufus 38, 14-116
    Thomas 55, 13-59
STANDIFER, Carrol 27, 20-1
    James E. 29, 20-3
    Shelton C. 65, 20-2
    W. L. 36, 17-1
    William C. 33, 20-3
STEP, Perry 50, 14-146
STEPHENS, Albert 4, 5-227
    Andrew 54, 4-192
    Bird 40, 14-151
    Isaac 31, 5-231
    Isaac 45, 13-73
    Jack 24, 12-26
    John 23, 5-230
    Mark 71, 5-222
    Mary 26, 5-227
    Moor 41, 9-147
    Roll 50, 5-221
    Sally 6, 5-227
    Sally 65, 6-272
    Sarah L. 16, 6-272
    W. E. 31, 17-4
    William 76, 13-71
    William H. 18, 6-272
STEPP, John 39, 14-108
STEWART, Delila 63, 19-8
    John 41, 19-7
    John E. 22, 19-1
    Robert 36, 19-7
STINSON, Mary 40, 17-7
    Sarah 11, 15-204
STONE, Patrick L. 32, 4-197
STONRY, Matildia 42, 10-195
STOUT, Elbert K. 28, 17-8
    John 61, 19-1
    Mary J. 32, 17-4
    William D. 42, 17-7
STRANAHAN, Charles C. 71, 19-3
SULLASS, John 30, 12-21
SULLIVAN, Buck 17, 12-48
    Franklin 41, 15-158
    Isaac 32, 4-165
    Matilda 30, 15-214
    Richard 17, 14-142
    William 65, 15-209
SUTHERLAND, Alexander 33, 15-186
    G. W. 48, 17-9
    James 29, 15-188
    John 56, 1-38
    Thomas 56, 15-189
SWAFFORD, A. E. 26, 7-4
    Aaron sr. 67, 10-183
    Aaron 43, 5-234
    Alaxander 55, 5-205
    Alex 29, 8-56
    Alfred 78, 6-280
    Alfred H. 26, 7-292
    Alfred K. 39, 6-282
    Anthony 16, 14-144
    C. 23, 10-167
    Clay 21, 7-296
    David 27, 5-210

SWAFFORD, Eliza 60, 5-211
    Green 54, 15-160
    Green 37, 10-196
    Henry 30, 4-201
    Hezekiah 22, 15-196
    Howard 40, 7-38
    Isaac E. 25, 6-253
    Isaac E. 53, 7-1
    J. D. 49, 9-104
    J. M. 51, 7-35
    James 73, 13-107
    James 20, 16-235
    James B. 34, 6-250
    Jeferson 60, 11-222
    John 34, 6-283
    L. 24, 11-218
    Lidie 70, 7-24
    Lucy 70, 6-290
    Mark 19, 14-131
    Mary E. 45, 5-206
    Matt 55, 10-184
    Nason 39, 6-291
    Peter J. 69, 4-203
    R. E. 22, 7-23
    Rachel 76, 4-192
    Rufus 26, 11-214
    S. H. L. 28, 8-76
    Samuel Jn. 37, 6-288
    Samuel Sn. 56, 6-285
    Samuel 24, 8-57
    Samuel 35, 12-43
    Sarah 16, 7-23
    Thomas 18, 12-36
    Thomas Y. 74, 6-289
SWEAT, George M. 37, 5-216
SWOFFORD, Jane 18, 12-42
SWOPE, George 10, 13-60
    James 15, 13-60
TAYLOR, Charles P. 35, 6-251
    Isaac N. 68, 6-252
TERRY, Mary Jane 57, 3-137
TETERS, James L. 34, 20-5
    John 39, 16-218
    William 16, 1-24
THOMAS, Jas. 47, 10-204
    William 53, 11-5
THOMPSON, Alfred 23, 15-194
    James 19, 11-7
    Leroy 45, 17-4
    Sarah 40, 12-18
THURMAN, Anderson 31, 10-203
    C. 24, 10-201
    Henry 25, 10-205
    Isaac 31, 15-205
    Isaac N. 42, 6-269
    J. C. 22, 7-20
    J. M. 51, 8-63
    Matilda J. 52, 17-5
    Richard 53, 5-212
    Saml. 30, 10-209
    W. A. 35, 16-3
    Wm. 56, 10-202
TILLEY, Edward F. 61, 5-239
    John 22, 5-240
    Robert N. 24, 5-241
TOLLETT, Elijah G. 52, 5-235
    Franklin 24, 6-267
    William 60, 5-227
TUCKER, Moses 58, 13-74
TUDOR, Landon 21, 6-254
TULLOP, Henry 29, 14-147
TULLOSO, James A. 70, 12-19
TULLOSS, Alfred 16, 16-1
    Jack 60, 13-100
    Johnathan 44, 12-50
TULLUS, James E. 40, 6-272
TURNER, John 39, 1-37
    John D. 29, 17-2
    Joseph 21, 3-123
    Kosouth 29, 17-2
    Mary 67, 16-4
    Samuel 19, 17-7
    Solomon 55, 2-79
    Thos. 37, 1-34
    William 25, 2-104
TWOFFORO?, James 50, 13-94
VANDERGRIFF, John 18, 19-6
VANHOY, Andy 18, 8-67

VANN, James M. 51, 16-240
VARNS, Arvazina 13, 1-9
    James 9, 1-9
    William M. 12, 1-9
VERNON, Caswell 50, 12-47
    Elizabeth 70, 14-109
    James A. 54, 14-144
    Martha 65, 14-109
VICKREY, Peter J. 22, 5-204
WADE, James M. 48, 6-266
WALKER, Benjamin F. 29, 18-7
    David H. 64, 4-180
    E. 35, 9-108
    Elizabeth 45, 5-214
    George 35, 8-71
    George W. 38, 18-2
    Isophine 50, 4-158
    James 65, 18-8
    Jeremiah 63, 18-1
    John 18, 13-93
    Mathew 24, 4-181
    Oliver 19, 13-93
    Rosalea 20, 8-75
    Stephen 45, 4-194
    William 35, 18-2
WALLING, Noah 24, 2-101
WARD, Elizabeth 22, 16-3
    John L. H. 72, 3-128
    John W. 32, 2-86
    Jonathan S. 40, 2-90
    Mary C. 7, 16-3
    Nancy M. 15, 3-117
    Sarah 6, 16-3
WARNER, Alfred 47, 4-176
WATKINS, Benjamin M. 30, 6-257
WEBB, George W. 29, 5-225
    Jane 26, 11-220
WELBORN, Joseph A. 16, 17-7
WELCH, John 26, 19-7
WETHERBEE, Henry 64, 14-134
WHALEY, Sarah 18, 1-32
    William L. L. 19, 1-22
WHITE, Clarisa 66, 1-22
    Daniel 78, 3-111
    Isaac E. 47, 3-109
    John P. 49, 3-110
    Rusel 70, 11-228
    Susan S. 60, 11-228
    William S. 45, 2-60
WHITTENBURG, Isaac 64, 12-56
    Jane 5, 12-49
    Joseph T. 30, 1-11
    Marla 5, 12-49
    Peter 28, 2-87
    Scott 35, 15-208
    Susan 73, 12-43
WILLIAMSON, Vavassor A. G. 24, 3-115
    William M. 53, 3-116
WILSOM?, Matildia 39, 8-89
WILSON, Charles 31, 15-169
    Joseph 20, 9-113
    Sallie 18, 8-84
    William G. 15, 6-289
WINSETT, William 38, 16-248
WITTEN, E. O. 43, 11-7
    Sada 16, 11-7
WOODS, S. A. 18, 9-124
WOOTON, Samuel 50, 15-193
WORTHINGTON, C. C. 32, 7-12
    David 35, 8-72
    Eli 24, 7-1
    Fred 28, 8-52
    Henry 35, 7-30
    Henry 21, 7-295
    Howard 45, 6-247
    J. C. 26, 7-45
    J. C. 49, 8-69
    J. F. 42, 7-18
    James jr. 50, 7-28
    Jas. 68, 7-44
    John 22, 8-65
    L. 30, 9-136
    Lewis 23, 15-161
    M. J. 44, 7-21
    Martin 29, 10-154
    R. B. 28, 8-55
    R. L. 24, 7-46

WORTHINGTON, Reuben 30, 11-7
    Reuben 45, 4-195
    S. P. 42, 7-14
    Washington 55, 7-47
    Wm. 75, 8-74
    Wm. 38, 11-243
WRIGHT, Joseph E. 30, 21-7
    Thos. 45, 10-210
WYATT, John 52, 4-185
WYERICK, J. A. 8, 11-231
WYOTT, John 22, 13-75
YATES, Mary 18, 10-172
    Thomas 25, 10-172
YEARGIN, Ada 10/12, 13-79
    Archey 6, 13-79
YOUNG, Florinda 9, 5-234
    Jesse 11, 5-234
    Melinda 16, 5-235
    Park 26, 5-243
ZIGLER, William 36, 16-220
_____, Lewis 25, 1-23

www.ingramcontent.com/pod-product-compliance
Lightning Source LLC
Chambersburg PA
CBHW080537090426
42733CB00015B/2609